GARDENING YOUR MIND
with
SPIRITUAL TOOLS

JOSEPH JONES

Copyright © 2024 Joseph Jones.

All rights reserved. No part of this book may be used or reproduced by any means, graphic, electronic, or mechanical, including photocopying, recording, taping or by any information storage retrieval system without the written permission of the author except in the case of brief quotations embodied in critical articles and reviews.

This book is a work of non-fiction. Unless otherwise noted, the author and the publisher make no explicit guarantees as to the accuracy of the information contained in this book and in some cases, names of people and places have been altered to protect their privacy.

WestBow Press books may be ordered through booksellers or by contacting:

WestBow Press
A Division of Thomas Nelson & Zondervan
1663 Liberty Drive
Bloomington, IN 47403
www.westbowpress.com
844-714-3454

Because of the dynamic nature of the Internet, any web addresses or links contained in this book may have changed since publication and may no longer be valid. The views expressed in this work are solely those of the author and do not necessarily reflect the views of the publisher, and the publisher hereby disclaims any responsibility for them.

Any people depicted in stock imagery provided by Getty Images are models, and such images are being used for illustrative purposes only.
Certain stock imagery © Getty Images.

ISBN: 979-8-3850-3694-3 (sc)
ISBN: 979-8-3850-3787-2 (hc)
ISBN: 979-8-3850-3695-0 (e)

Library of Congress Control Number: 2024922537

Print information available on the last page.

WestBow Press rev. date: 11/05/2024

The reward of a thing well done is having done it.
—Ralph Waldo Emerson

The garden of the world has no limits, except in your mind.
—Rumi

The mind is everything. What you think, you become.
—Buddha

To my son, Jonathan Leander Jones, who passed away from this life in July 2018. His spirit lives on in my heart.

To my wife, Mona, who started this journey with me as a friend, who believed in me, and who saw me as marriage material.

To my parents, Lillian and Ester Jones, who taught me to never be afraid of doing a hard day's work.

To my brothers, Eddie and Randy, who have passed away. I miss them dearly.

To my siblings, Kenny, Lula, Betty, Linda and Lonny for their love and support.

Finally, to my daughter, Jenell, and all my grandchildren, especially my nonverbal autistic grandson, Gavin, my buddy, who at the time of drafting this book was beginning to sing "Now I Know My ABCs" at nine years old. Thank you, Lord.

CONTENTS

Foreword xi
Preface..xiii
Acknowledgments xix
Introduction xxi

Garden Tools/Spiritual Meaning 1
Tending the Garden Within with Spiritual Tools............................. 4
Embracing Change and Transformation 6
You Can Tell a Tree by the Fruit It Bears.. 10
Transcending Ego: The Path to Spiritual Awakening.................... 15
Cultivating Positive Thoughts and Mindset 22
Seed to Plant..26
Embracing Self-Love and Discernment 35
Inner Growth and Transformation 38
Acceptance and Surrender 44
Embracing Courage and Resilience 46
Learning to Love 54
Harvesting Inner Peace 56
Gateway to Connecting to a Higher Consciousness......................63
Uncertainty: Every Storm Is Not in the Forecast 65
Seed of Inspiration 67
Stopping the War Within...69

References 73

FOREWORD

Dear Joseph,

As I sit down to pen these words, I reflect on the incredible journey we have shared for over four decades as friends and now as husband and wife. I am filled with a deep sense of gratitude and admiration for the strength, love, and guidance that have been the cornerstone of your success—from overcoming adversity to rising through the ranks from unemployment to the helm of our company.

Your dedication to personal growth and spiritual development has transformed your life and been a beacon of light for those around you, including me. Your journey to recovery from addiction, spanning over thirty-five years, stands as a testament to your resilience and unwavering commitment to self-improvement.

In this foreword, I am honored to share with the world the profound impact you have had on my life and the invaluable lessons we have learned together. Your insights on nurturing the mind with spiritual tools are not just words on a page but a testament to a life well-lived and a love that knows no bounds.

With love and admiration
Mona Jones

PREFACE

In the profound journey depicted within the pages of *Gardening Your Mind with Spiritual Tools*, I hope these words resonate with the poignant echoes of my losses, desperation, and spiritual adversities. The weight of unbearable sorrow from the death of my only son, combined with the suffocating grip of isolation and the throes of hopelessness, paints a raw and unflinchingly honest portrait of being at one's wits end.

Amidst the tumultuous storm of emotions, I want to candidly explore navigating spiritual hostility and emotional dishonesty to offer a glimmer of light in the darkness. Through the transformative power of spiritual tools and unwavering resilience, the narrative unfolds as a testament to the human spirit's capacity to rise from the ashes of despair.

Within these pages, the fusion of spirituality and recovery from addiction becomes not just a lifeline but a beacon of hope amidst the darkest of nights. As you immerse yourself in this poignant tale of redemption and renewal, you may find solace, inspiration, and the courage to embark on your journey toward healing and inner peace.

Step into the realm of *Gardening Your Mind with Spiritual Tools*. When self-doubt weighs heavy on your spirit, emotions whirl out of control, dishonesty clouds your spiritual clarity, and life feels unfair, it's easy to feel lost in the whirlwind of life's challenges. This book stands as a beacon of hope, offering a nurturing sanctuary where I will assist you in cultivating your self-worth, bringing harmony to your emotional landscape, and restoring integrity to your spiritual core.

Within these pages, you will embark on a profound journey of self-discovery and healing. Together, we will tend the soil of your mind, planting seeds of empowerment and resilience that will weather even the harshest emotional storms. Through mindful reflection, practical tools, and heartfelt guidance, this book will empower you to reclaim your inner strength, find peace amidst the chaos, and rediscover the beauty of your authentic self.

Let's walk this path of transformation hand in hand, tending to the garden of your mind with care and compassion. As you delve into *Gardening Your Mind with Spiritual Tools*, may you integrate solace, clarity, and the unwavering belief that healing and growth are always within reach, no matter how turbulent the journey may seem. The lack of integration of the natural human growth process causes trauma. I learned the difference between my values, beliefs, and rules. While the three are different from each other, they are also very much related and intertwined to form me. Values, beliefs, and rules sit on top of each other, with values forming the base of the pyramid structure, beliefs in the middle, and rules at the top of the stack. The lack of integration of the natural human growth process can cause trauma as individuals may struggle to develop a cohesive sense of self and identity. When values, beliefs, and rules are not integrated effectively, it can lead to internal conflicts, confusion, and a lack of direction in one's life. Values serve as the foundation of one's identity, shaping one's core principles and guiding principles. Beliefs, positioned in the middle, represent the thoughts and convictions that individuals hold about themselves and the world around them. Rules, situated at the top, are the external guidelines and regulations that individuals follow based on their values and beliefs. When these aspects are not aligned or integrated properly, individuals may experience inner turmoil, cognitive dissonance, and a sense of disconnect, which can contribute to emotional distress and psychological trauma.

Traumatized at Developmental Stages

1. Seedling stage: Early childhood trauma is akin to a young seedling exposed to harsh conditions such as a storm or drought. Just like a young plant that struggles to grow strong roots in adverse

conditions, a child experiencing trauma may struggle to develop a secure emotional foundation.
2. Impact: This can lead to vulnerability and undernourished emotional development, making it hard to thrive later in life.

Emotionally Suppressive

1. Stagnant soil: Emotionally suppressive soil is comparable to compacted soil lacking aeration. Emotions, like nutrients, cannot circulate freely, leading to a stunted growth environment.
2. Impact: Just as plants need healthy soil to grow, humans need emotional expression to develop healthily. Repression prevents the natural flow of emotions, which can result in poor mental health and stunted emotional growth.

Spiritually Unfriendly

1. Toxic chemicals: A spiritually hostile environment can be likened to applying toxic chemicals to a garden. These chemicals can damage plants and soil, making growth almost impossible.
2. Impact: Exposure to such toxicity can close off spiritual pathways, preventing the inner growth necessary for holistic well-being. Healing becomes more challenging in a spiritually hostile environment.

Dysfunctional Environment

1. Neglected garden: A dysfunctional environment is like a neglected garden overrun with weeds and pests. Without proper care and maintenance, the garden cannot thrive.
2. Impact: Individuals cannot reach their full potential in a dysfunctional home or community. Destructive patterns and negative influences stifle growth and reinforce trauma, leading to further emotional and spiritual instability.

Development Process

Throughout every stage of my growth, I experienced trauma. I lived in an environment that was emotionally suppressive, spiritually unfriendly, and dysfunctional. As I moved to the next stage, I felt incomplete and unprepared, which led to more trauma, wounded again and again through life experiences, disappointment, and failures.

I was unable to own and honor my true feelings and beliefs out of my shame of being different from others, always seeking approval and validation from others but feeling isolated and disconnected. At fifteen, I became a father, and while the initial joy was exciting, it swiftly turned into turmoil when my girlfriend sought other men attention and affection. Faced with rejection and competition, I spiraled into anger and despair, gravitating toward alcohol as a source of comfort and courage. I wandered through life recklessly, seeking purpose and meaning, only to be consumed by drugs and alcohol in a desperate attempt to numb the pain and escape the disappointments that plagued my existence.

This turbulent path led to addiction, unemployment, homelessness, the end of the relationship and the heart-wrenching loss of loved ones, each experience taking a heavy toll on my spirit. Yet, through the guiding spiritual principles of Alcoholics Anonymous (AA) and Narcotics Anonymous (NA), I began to reclaim my life. These twelve-step programs became a lifeline, sparking profound healing for my mind, body, and soul.

As I learned to trust in a higher power, my transformation began. I realized how I had unknowingly blocked myself from this power of healing. By neglecting to place God first in my life, I had deprived myself of the very help I sought. It dawned on me that problems cannot be solved from the same mindset that created them. My journey is now about illuminating the hallways of my life, understanding that as one door closes, another opens.

Through the transformative power of spiritual reprogramming, I discovered the ability to operate from a higher consciousness. I learned to nurture my mind and cultivate inner resilience in the face of life's overwhelming challenges. This journey is about conflict resolution, maintaining sanity in an insane world, embracing a new normal, and sharing my personal experiences with others. By exposing my fears and past wounds, I found healing—a transition that opened me to a new source of power and possibility.

ACKNOWLEDGMENTS

I want to express my profound gratitude for others' mentorship and guidance. Dr. Wendell James and Dr. Alretta Tolbert, owner and program director of Adult Educational Technologies in Mental Health Services, have both inspired and transformed my career into providing a fulfilling journey I could not have imagined for myself. Their wisdom, support, and encouragement have been invaluable and shaped me into the professional I am today. I give thanks to my childhood friend and mentor, Dr. Glenester Irvin, in Mental Health Services through Positive Links.

Finally, I give thanks to all my friends in twelve-step programs.

INTRODUCTION

Imagine the mind and a garden as parallel concepts that thrive through care and attention. Just like a garden needs nourishment from the sun, pruning, and protection to bloom, our minds also require nurturing through positive thoughts, learning, and self-reflection to grow and flourish. The parallel between planting seeds in a garden and planting ideas or knowledge in our minds illustrates the importance of patience and diligence in both processes.

Dive into this transformational journey where the seeds of mindfulness, the roots of self-discovery, and the blossoms of inner peace intertwine. Explore how tending to your mind resembles a garden, cultivating growth and blooming spiritual abundance. Discover the power of merging practical gardening tips with profound spiritual tools to nurture your soul and cultivate a vibrant inner landscape.

Unlock the secrets of your inner garden and watch your soul bloom! In *Gardening Your Mind with Spiritual Tools*, you will uncover a unique blend of ancient wisdom and practical insights to cultivate a bountiful mind. Just as a gardener tends to plants with care and intention, discover how to nurture your thoughts, plant seeds of positivity, and prune away negativity. Get ready to embark on a soul-stirring journey where every page unveils the beauty of spiritual growth within your mental landscape. Your mind is the garden. Are you ready to sow the seeds of transformation?

As we explore navigating through life changes from a spiritual perspective in life under new management, consider the following personalized approaches.

Like a garden, your mind can be nurtured and cultivated to grow beautiful thoughts and ideas. Both require care, attention, and patience to flourish and reach their full potential.

Are you ready to embark on a holistic growth and spiritual blossoming journey? Let's get ready to dig deep together.

GARDEN TOOLS/ SPIRITUAL MEANING

The following are spiritual parallels and meanings for each gardening tool. Not all tools will be used in the book. Some will be explained in the upcoming workbook.

1. **Hand trowel** symbolizes precision and attention to detail in our spiritual growth, digging deep to uncover hidden truths.
2. **Spade** represents the foundation of our spiritual journey, turning over soil and old beliefs to plant new seeds of wisdom.
3. **Shovel** signifies digging deep within us to unearth buried emotions and experiences for healing.
4. **Garden fork** symbolizes breaking up stagnant energy within us, allowing for growth and expansion in our spiritual practice.
5. **Pruning shears** represent letting go of what no longer serves us, trimming away habits or thoughts that hinder our spiritual progress.
6. **Hedge shears** signify shaping boundaries in our spiritual lives, creating a sense of protection and clarity in our practices.
7. **Loppers** symbolize cutting away negative influences in our spiritual environment, fostering space for positivity and growth.
8. **Garden rake** represents leveling and smoothing the bumps in our spiritual path, creating harmony and balance within.
9. **Leaf rake** symbolizes the act of gathering and releasing what is no longer needed in our spiritual journey, clearing space for new growth.
10. **Wheelbarrow** signifies carrying the burdens of our spiritual transformation with grace and strength, moving forward with purpose.

11. **Garden hoe** represents cultivating our inner soil, preparing it for the seeds of insight and understanding.
12. **Weeder** symbolizes uprooting weeds of doubt and fear from our spiritual gardens, making space for the flowers of faith to bloom.
13. **Garden knife** signifies cutting through illusions and falsehoods on our spiritual path, seeking clarity and truth.
14. **Garden scissors** represent fine-tuning our spiritual practices, trimming away excess to focus on what truly matters.
15. **Soil knife** symbolizes the deep connection between our spiritual growth and the nourishing earth, grounding us in our journey.
16. **Watering can** or **garden hose** signifies the flow of spiritual energy and love into our lives, nourishing our growth and inner balance.
17. **Sprinkler** represents the gentle shower of blessings and abundance in our spiritual practice, refreshing and revitalizing our spirit.
18. **Garden gloves** symbolize protection and resilience in our spiritual work, shielding us from harm as we tend to our inner garden.
19. **Kneepads** signify humility and surrender in our spiritual endeavors, reminding us to kneel in gratitude and service.
20. **Pruning saw** represents cutting through tough obstacles on our spiritual path, clearing the way for new possibilities.
21. **Machete** or **clearing sickle** symbolizes cutting through dense undergrowth in our spiritual journey, clearing a path to clarity and vision.
22. **Cultivator** signifies the continuous effort and dedication required in our spiritual growth, tilling the soil of our souls for lasting transformation.
23. **Bulb planter** represents planting seeds of intention in our spiritual garden, nurturing them with care and patience.
24. **Soil scoop** symbolizes digging deep into our spiritual essence, uncovering hidden treasures and insights.
25. **Plant stakes and ties** signify the support and connections we rely on in our spiritual journey, anchoring us in times of growth and change.
26. **Gardening apron** symbolizes preparing oneself for spiritual work, embracing the responsibilities and joys of tending to the inner garden with care and dedication.

27. **Seed packets** represent the intentions and aspirations we plant in our spiritual practice, with each seed carrying the potential for growth and transformation.
28. **Compost bin** signifies transforming challenges and setbacks into fertile ground for spiritual growth and renewal.
29. **Garden cart** symbolizes the journey of gathering wisdom and experiences on our spiritual path, carrying them forward to nurture our inner landscape.
30. **Sun hat** represents the protection and guidance we seek from higher sources during our spiritual journey, shielding us from harmful influences.
31. **Garden kneeler bench** signifies kneeling in prayer or meditation, grounding ourselves in humility and connection to the divine.
32. **Trellis** symbolizes the structure and support we build in our spiritual practice, guiding our growth upward toward enlightenment.
33. **Garden lantern** represents illuminating our inner darkness with the light of spiritual wisdom, guiding us through challenges and shadows.
34. **Bird feeder** signifies nurturing our spiritual connections with others, fostering community, and sharing in the abundance of spiritual insights.
35. **Wind chimes** symbolize the flow of spiritual energy and vibrations through our environment, harmonizing our inner and outer worlds.
36. **Reflective garden sphere** represents the act of self-reflection and introspection on our spiritual journey, gaining clarity and insight through contemplation.
37. **Pathway stones** signify the steps we take along our spiritual path, with each stone representing a lesson or milestone in our personal evolution.
38. **Garden sanctuary** symbolizes creating a sacred space for inner reflection and meditation, cultivating peace and tranquility within.
39. **Rain barrel** represents the abundance of spiritual blessings and insights we gather along our journey, storing them for future growth and nourishment.
40. **Zen garden sand rake** signifies the practice of mindfulness and focus on our spiritual work, creating patterns of serenity and balance in the mind.

TENDING THE GARDEN WITHIN WITH SPIRITUAL TOOLS

> The Soul has no secret that the behavior does not reveal.
> —Lao Tzu, Chinese philosopher

Let's get started!

Soul Searching

The key to healing our wounded souls is getting transparent and honest in our human emotional process. Until we can do this—until we change the twisted, distorted, negative perspectives and reactions to our human emotions that are a result of having been born into and grown up in a dysfunctional, emotionally repressive, spiritually hostile environment—we cannot get in touch with the level of emotional energy that is our truth. We cannot get in touch with or reconnect to our spiritual selves.

Each of us has an inner channel to truth, an inner channel to the Great Spirit. But that inner channel is blocked by suppressed emotional energy, twisted, distorted attitudes, and false beliefs.

We can intellectually throw out false beliefs. We can intellectually remember and embrace the truth of oneness, light, and love. But we cannot integrate spiritual truths into our day-to-day human existence in a way that allows us to change the dysfunctional behavior patterns that we had to adopt to survive until we deal with our emotional wounds, until we deal with the subconscious emotional programming from our childhoods.

- I could not learn to love without honestly owning my rage!
- We cannot allow ourselves to be truly intimate with ourselves or anyone else without owning our grief.
- We cannot clearly reconnect with the light unless we are willing to own and honor our experience in darkness.
- We cannot fully feel the joy unless we are willing to feel the sadness.

We need to do our emotional healing to heal our wounded souls, reconnect with our souls on the highest consciousness levels, and reconnect with the God-Force, the Universal Spirit that is love, light, joy, and truth. By reprogramming our minds, we can operate with an expanded consciousness with fewer abusive tools (Burney 1995).

EMBRACING CHANGE AND TRANSFORMATION

Tools Needed

1. **Pruning shears** symbolize cutting away unproductive or harmful aspects of your life, such as negative thoughts, toxic relationships, or unhealthy habits. Just as pruning shears help a plant grow healthier by removing dead or overgrown branches, embracing the practice can lead to personal growth and transformation.
2. **Trowel** digs into the soil, representing delving deep into your feelings, thoughts, and experiences. By examining and understanding these deeper layers, you can plant innovative ideas or behaviors to aid in your development and change.
3. **Watering can** symbolizes nurturing and consistently supporting new positive habits, goals, or mindsets. Just as plants need regular watering to thrive, sustaining your growth requires ongoing effort and attention.

A mind untended is like a garden untended. "A mind left neglected is like a soul without nurturing". I cannot emphasize the importance of tending to and caring for one's mind just as one would care for a garden. Nourish the soul for spiritual growth.

We begin our journey with the caterpillar metamorphosis. The concept of the caterpillar's transformation into a butterfly as a metaphor for personal growth and spiritual evolution is a narrative from the caterpillar's experience.

The Body

The Caterpillar's Perspective

- We observe the caterpillar's experience of going through what may seem like the end of the world as it enters the chrysalis stage.
- The feelings of confusion, confinement, and darkness that may parallel our own struggles with change and uncertainty must make one want to die.

Divine Intervention

- We reflect on the idea that sometimes what appears to be the end is a new beginning, guided by a higher power or universal force.
- The caterpillar's transformation into a butterfly is seen as a miraculous act of creation, which is the perfect plan of God because I am here to play the role God assigns me to without my permission.

Embracing Transformation

- Embrace change and trust in the process of transformation, even when it feels challenging or uncomfortable.
- Let go of what is familiar: beliefs, habits, and self-defeating talk. Being in the void leads you through the unfamiliar, for example, death, divorce, separation, retirement, or any ending. The void is a time of not knowing. It may feel like a state of not doing, of nothingness. Only when you stop knowing in your normal way and experience not knowing can you connect with new knowledge! This state of nothingness and not knowing is a state of being rather than doing, of stillness and silence. Many of you fear the void because it offers neither a solid foundation nor a clear identity. What you have identified with may be changing to allow you to grow into a greater identity (Roman 1988).
- Practical spiritual tools and practices support individuals in navigating periods of change and reinvention. A spiritual tool is a nonmaterial practice or technique that can be utilized at any given time (when willing) that can promote a change in one's attitude, outlook, self-awakening, and quality of life.

The Emergence of the Butterfly

- The butterfly's emergence from the chrysalis is a powerful metaphor for personal growth, self-realization, and spiritual rebirth. 1 Corinthians 15:31 (KJV) reads, "One must die as I know myself to be reborn" (Bible n.d.). Be present for life in the here and now. Soar over issues and learn your inner power. Learn to go with the natural flow of life without being at war with it.

Experience the beauty, freedom, and resilience of life that come with embracing one's true potential. Take time to connect with people, nature, animals, and anything that brings you out of isolation. Being in a non-shaming environment has helped me escape the isolation of uniqueness.

Conclusion

The following are the main lessons learned from the caterpillar's journey to becoming a butterfly: the importance of faith, patience, and inner strength in times of transformation.

The journey of a caterpillar to butterfly teaches us the importance of embracing change, trusting the process, and realizing our potential for transformation. It reminds us that growth often involves periods of struggle and discomfort, but these challenges lead to a beautiful outcome. This metamorphosis can symbolize personal growth, resilience, and the beauty of embracing new beginnings.

I have learned to see change as an opportunity for growth and spiritual awakening, to cultivate my own wings to soar to new heights in understanding my relationship with God, myself, and life. I learned to relate to my inner healing process from a reversed perspective. I was trained to be emotionally dishonest, that is, to not feel the feelings or go to the other extreme by allowing the feelings to totally run my life and give power to, to buy into, the reversed attitudes. So it is shameful to be human; it is bad to make mistakes. God is punishing and judgmental. To find balance within, I had to change my relationship with my inner process by being honest.

I needed to learn how to set boundaries within, both emotionally and intellectually, by integrating spiritual truth into my process. Because "I feel like a failure" does not mean that is the truth. The spiritual truth is that failure is an opportunity for growth. I can set a boundary with my emotions by not buying into the illusion that what I am feeling is who I am. I can set a boundary intellectually by telling that part of my mind that is judging and shaming me to shut up because that is my dis-ease lying to me. I can feel and release the emotional pain energy at the same time I am telling myself the truth by not buying into the shame and judgment (Burney 1995).

I never despise humble beginnings. I do not take for granted that I know how my chance for greatest should look. If I did, I would already be doing it or having it.

YOU CAN TELL A TREE BY THE FRUIT IT BEARS

How do you stand in your garden?

- Assertive communicator: Assertive communication involves expressing your thoughts, feelings, and needs directly and respectfully. For example, "I feel uncomfortable with the current situation, and I would appreciate it if we could discuss how to improve it."
- Passive communicator: Passive communication involves avoiding expressing one's own thoughts and feelings, often resulting in passivity and compliance, for example, remaining silent when you disagree with something to avoid confrontation.
- Aggressive communicator: Aggressive communication involves expressing one's thoughts and feelings in a way that disregards the rights of others, for example, yelling, insulting, or belittling someone during a disagreement.
- Passive-aggressive communicator: Passive-aggressive communication involves indirectly expressing hostility or resentment, for example, agreeing to do something with a smile but purposely doing it inadequately.
- Collaborative communicator: Collaborative communication involves working together to find mutually beneficial solutions or outcomes, for example, brainstorming ideas with a team to reach a consensus on a project.

- Transactional communicator: Transactional communication focuses on the exchange of information to achieve a specific goal, for example, sending emails to coordinate tasks and updates with colleagues.
- Transformational communicator: Transformational communication aims to inspire and motivate others to achieve a common goal through effective communication and leadership, for example, a leader who motivates their team by articulating a compelling vision.

A large part of what we identify as our personality is in fact a distorted view of who we really are due to the type of behavioral defenses we have adopted to fit the role(s) we were forced to assume according to the dynamics of our family structure.

Behavioral Defenses

These behavioral defenses suggest we adopt different degrees and combinations of these distinct types of behaviors as our personal defense system, and we swing from one extreme to the other within our personal spectrum.

The Relentless Steamroller: The Aggressive-Aggressive Defense

In the garden of the mind, certain defenses can act like relentless steamrollers, forcefully flattening down everything in their path without consideration for the well-being of others. This defense mechanism is often exhibited by individuals who display what we call the "aggressive-aggressive defense."

These individuals, often counter-independent, adopt an attitude of "I don't care what anyone thinks." Like a steamroller, they push through and overpower others, justifying their actions by asserting that you deserve it. This mentality mirrors a "survival of the fittest" approach, frequently seen in hard-driving capitalists or self-righteous zealots who feel superior to most everyone else.

Such individuals typically despise what they perceive as weakness in others, which actually reflects their own deep-seated fear and shame regarding their humanity. This aggressive stance is a protective mechanism, a spiritual tool-turned-weapon they use to guard against their vulnerabilities and insecurities.

Understanding this type of defense mechanism is crucial in the spiritual gardening of the mind. By recognizing the roots of this aggression—fear and shame—we can begin to cultivate compassion, both for ourselves and those who exhibit such behaviors. Employing tools like mindfulness, empathy, and self-reflection, we can transform this relentless steamrolling into more constructive and nurturing behaviors, promoting a healthier, more harmonious mental garden.

The Self-Sacrificing Steamroller: The Aggressive-Passive Defense

In the garden of the mind, certain defense mechanisms can act like invasive species, overpowering the balance and harmony of the environment. One such mechanism is exhibited by individuals who display the "aggressive-passive defense," also known as the "self-sacrificing bulldozer."

These individuals will run you down, metaphorically speaking, and then claim they did it for your own good, insisting it hurt them more than it did you. They aggressively try to control others under the guise of knowing what is right and what one should do, feeling an overwhelming sense of obligation to inform and correct.

Self-sacrificing bulldozers are perpetually setting themselves up to be the perpetrator because they believe others do not do things the right way, in other words, their way. This behavior stems from a combination of deep-seated control issues, a need for superiority, and an inflated sense of responsibility for others' actions.

Understanding this defense mechanism is crucial in the spiritual gardening of the mind. By recognizing the roots of aggressive-passive behaviors—often a combination of fear, insecurity, and a compulsion to impose one's will—we can begin to cultivate healthier interactions. Employing spiritual tools like compassion, active listening, and boundary-setting, we can transform these toxic dynamics into more balanced and respectful relationships. This cultivation promotes a healthier, more harmonious mental garden where mutual respect and understanding can flourish.

The Militant Martyr: The Passive-Aggressive Defense

In the garden of the mind, certain defense mechanisms can act like insidious weeds, quietly strangling the life out of other healthy plants. This phenomenon is often seen in individuals who exhibit what we call the "passive-aggressive defense," or the "militant martyr."

These individuals smile sweetly while emotionally cutting others to pieces with their seemingly innocent, double-edged remarks. They attempt to control others "for their own good," but their methods are covert and passive-aggressive. Under the guise of wanting the best for you, they sabotage at every opportunity.

Militant martyrs perceive themselves as benevolent individuals, continually and unfairly victimized by their ungrateful loved ones. This sense of victimization dominates their conversations and focus, revealing a profound self-absorption. Their fixation on their own perceived martyrdom makes it nearly impossible for them to truly hear or empathize with what others are saying.

Understanding this defense mechanism is crucial in the spiritual gardening of the mind. By recognizing the origins of passive-aggressive behaviors—often a mix of fear, insecurity, and a need for control—we can begin to cultivate empathy and self-awareness. Employing spiritual tools like active listening, genuine compassion, and meaningful self-reflection, we can transform these covert behaviors into more open and supportive interactions. This shift promotes a healthier, more harmonious mental garden where trust and understanding can flourish.

The Self-Sacrificing Martyr:
The Passive-Passive Defense

In the garden of the mind, certain defense mechanisms can serve as pervasive shadows that stifle growth and vitality. One such shadow is exhibited by individuals who display the "passive-passive defense," also known as the "self-sacrificing martyr."

These individuals spend so much time and energy demeaning themselves and projecting an image of emotional fragility that anyone who even thinks of becoming upset with them feels an overwhelming sense of guilt. They possess incredibly accurate, long-range, stealth guilt torpedoes that remain effective even long after their passing.

For the self-sacrificing martyr, guilt is akin to the primary defense mechanism of a skunk's stink. Just as a skunk uses its pungent scent to ward off threats, these individuals use guilt to control and manipulate their surroundings. This pervasive guilt serves as a barrier, preventing others from addressing the underlying issues and fostering an environment of emotional manipulation.

Understanding this defense mechanism is crucial in the spiritual gardening of the mind. By recognizing the roots of self-sacrificing behaviors—often a mix of deep-seated insecurities, a need for validation, and fear of confrontation—we can begin to cultivate healthier interactions. Employing spiritual tools like self-compassion, assertiveness training, and constructive communication, we can transform these toxic dynamics into more transparent and supportive relationships. This cultivation promotes a healthier, more harmonious mental garden where accountability and mutual respect can thrive.

These are all defense systems adopted out of necessity to survive. They are all defensive disguises whose purpose is to protect the wounded, terrified child within (Burney 1995).

TRANSCENDING EGO: THE PATH TO SPIRITUAL AWAKENING

Tools Needed

- **Shovel** digs deep into your subconscious and unearthing hidden truths. This represents the deep digging required to uncover hidden truths and profound insights within yourself. Just as a shovel helps you dig through layers of soil to reach deeper levels, you use introspection and meditation to unearth deeper spiritual understandings and connect with your inner self.
- **Hoe** clears out distractions and unnecessary clutter in your mind. This symbolizes the clearing away of distractions and mental clutter that prevent spiritual growth. Just as a hoe removes weeds and prepares the ground for planting, you need to eliminate negative thoughts, doubts, and external distractions to create a clear and fertile environment for spiritual growth.
- **Garden fork** breaks up and aerates the soil of your beliefs, allowing new spiritual insights to take root and grow. This tool breaks up and aerates compacted soil, allowing water and nutrients to penetrate more easily. Metaphorically, it represents breaking up rigid beliefs and preconceptions in your mind, making way for new spiritual insights and growth. By loosening the soil of your spirit, you allow current ideas and perspectives to flourish.

The concept of the ego is the sense of individual identity and separation from the divine. It's the significance of letting go of ego for spiritual growth. I cannot be separated from my Creator; it just feels like separation.

Understanding the Ego

The ego is the part of our psyche that seeks validation, control, and self-preservation, often leading to fear, attachment, and suffering. The ego can be described as the voice in our mind that constantly craves approval, tries to control situations, and prioritizes self-protection. It often brings about feelings of fear, attachment to outcomes, and unnecessary suffering and shame. I explored how the ego can hinder my spiritual evolution by creating barriers to connecting with my higher self or the divine spirit.

The ego acts like a protective barrier that can block my ability to connect with my inner wisdom or a higher power. It does this by constantly seeking validation, control, and self-preservation, which can cloud my judgment and lead me to make decisions based on fear, insecurities, and selfish desires. This focus on the self can prevent me from experiencing true spiritual growth and connection, as it keeps me trapped in my own limited perspective rather than opening to the broader, interconnected universe around me. By letting go of ego-driven tendencies, I can create space for deeper connections with my higher self and the divine, allowing me to experience greater peace, purpose, and fulfillment in my spiritual journey.

The Death of the Ego

Tools Needed

- **Compost bin** represents the process of taking old, unhelpful aspects of your ego and transforming them into something beneficial. Just as a compost bin turns organic waste into nutrient-rich soil, you can reprocess parts of your ego that no longer serve you, transforming them into valuable lessons and strengths that enrich your personal growth.

- **Secateurs**, small pruning tools, symbolize the precise cutting away of excessive self-importance, arrogance, and overinflated ego. Much like how secateurs trim back unnecessary growth to promote the health of a plant, you can use self-reflection and humility to trim back parts of your ego that hinder genuine self-awareness and compassion.
- **Spade** represents the action of turning over and renewing the soil of your mind. By digging deep and turning over the old, hard layers, you create a fresh, fertile ground for new thoughts and behaviors that align with humility and self-awareness. This process helps to dismantle the ego, allowing more authentic and meaningful personal growth to take root.

Experiencing the transformative process of releasing the ego's grip on my thoughts, emotions, and actions, often referred to as the "death of the ego," can feel like the end of the world. This involves letting go of my tendencies to constantly seek validation, control situations, and act from a place of fear and self-centeredness. It means becoming aware of my ego-driven thoughts, emotions, and actions and consciously choosing to detach from them. This process allows me to cultivate a greater sense of self-awareness, humility, and compassion toward myself and others. I create space for more authentic and heart-centered ways of thinking, feeling, and behaving, leading to a deeper sense of inner peace, harmony, and connection with my higher self and the world around me by releasing the ego's grip.

I will examine the challenges and resistance that could happen when confronting and transcending egoic patterns and beliefs. When confronting and transcending egoic patterns and beliefs, challenges and resistance could happen due to the ego's instinct to protect itself and maintain the status quo. Some common obstacles include:

- Fear of the unknown: The ego prefers familiarity and predictability, so stepping into the unknown or challenging existing beliefs can trigger fear and anxiety.
- Attachment to identity: The ego forms a sense of self based on past experiences and beliefs. Letting go of these identities can be uncomfortable and threatening to the ego's sense of security.

- Inner resistance: The ego resists change and growth because it disrupts the ego's established patterns and control over one's thoughts, emotions, and actions.
- Judgment and self-criticism: The ego often fuels self-judgment and criticism, making it difficult to have compassion and patience with oneself during the process of transcending egoic patterns.
- External influences: Society, culture, and relationships can reinforce egoic behaviors and beliefs, creating additional challenges in breaking free from these patterns.

By acknowledging and understanding these challenges and resistance, individuals can embrace the process of transcending ego with patience, self-compassion, and a willingness to embrace discomfort as part of the journey toward greater self-awareness and spiritual growth.

Surrender and Letting Go

Explore the practices of surrender, acceptance, and letting go as ways to release ego identification and cultivate inner peace and spiritual alignment.

Practicing, training, and rehearsing the act of surrendering, accepting, and letting go involves learning to release the need for controlling outcomes and validation that the ego craves. Surrendering means trusting that things will unfold as they are meant to, even if it is different from what we expect. Acceptance is about acknowledging and making peace with things as they are rather than resisting or fighting against them. Letting go is the process of detaching from ego-driven desires and attachments, allowing us to move forward with a sense of freedom and openness.

These practices help us loosen the ego's grip, cultivate a more peaceful and centered state of mind, and align ourselves with deeper spiritual truths and values. By practicing surrender, acceptance, and letting go, we can experience greater inner peace, clarity, and harmony in our lives.

Tools and techniques such as meditation, mindfulness, and self-inquiry can help individuals detach from ego-driven narratives.

- Meditation: Take a few minutes each day to sit quietly, focus on your breath, and observe your thoughts without judgment. This practice helps create space between you and your ego, allowing you to cultivate inner peace and clarity.
- Mindfulness: Stay present in the moment by paying attention to your thoughts, emotions, and sensations without getting caught up in them. Mindfulness helps you become aware of your ego's patterns and reactions, enabling you to respond consciously rather than reactively.
- Self-inquiry: Ask yourself reflective questions to explore your beliefs, motivations, and reactions, for example, "Why do I feel this way?" or "Is this thought true?" Self-inquiry helps you uncover and challenge ego-driven narratives, leading to greater self-awareness and insight.

By incorporating these tools into your daily routine, you can gradually disengage from ego-driven narratives, cultivate a deeper connection with your true self, and navigate life with more clarity, authenticity, and peace.

Rebirth and Spiritual Life

By illustrating the liberation and clarity that comes with transcending ego, you can embrace a more authentic, heart-centered way of being. Transcending the ego and embracing a more authentic, heart-centered way of being can bring about a sense of liberation and clarity in the following ways:

- Freedom from inner conflict: Letting go of ego-driven insecurities, fears, and attachments can bring a sense of inner peace and freedom from constant mental chatter and self-doubt. This means I am not at war with myself.
- Heightened awareness: Embracing a heart-centered approach can help you become more attuned to your true desires, values, and intuition, allowing you to make decisions from a place of clarity and authenticity. I am operating from a higher consciousness.

- Deeper connections: By releasing egoic barriers, you can cultivate stronger and more meaningful relationships based on empathy, compassion, and genuine connection with others.
- Increased joy and fulfillment: Living from a heart-centered place can lead to a deeper sense of joy, gratitude, and fulfillment as you align with your purpose and live in harmony with your values and intentions.

Overall, transcending the ego and embracing an authentic, heart-centered way of being can bring about a profound shift in how you experience life, opening doors to deeper understanding, connection, and fulfillment in your personal and spiritual journey.

Personal stories, insights, and teachings illustrate the profound shift from egoic living to a more spiritually aligned and purposeful existence.

Learning to go with the natural flow of life and seeing change as an opportunity for growth is a result of more time with Father God, just like a child spends time with their parent. This is a relationship unlike going to church once a week on Sunday. It's not much of a relationship if you see your child for a few hours on Sunday. Right!

Conclusion

The chapter's key teachings are on transcending ego and embracing a spiritual life rooted in love, presence, and interconnectedness. Empower yourself to embark on your own journey of ego dissolution, inviting you to deepen your spiritual practice and embody your true essence beyond the confines of the ego.

The void of being a caterpillar is a state of consciousness; it is the start of the transformation. I must die as I know myself to be reborn with spiritual awareness. By going into a state of not being the me that lacks or is not worthy, I can expand beyond my current limits, letting go of old ideas, and move to the next level of growth without telling myself how it should be. In the void, you leave behind familiar structures, habits, thoughts, behaviors, and attitudes and go deep within to create new ones that match your higher vibration. In this state, you can receive insights and do inner work. It can last for minutes, hours, days, or even weeks. However, it is important to replace self-defeating habits with empowering self-supporting habits. As you practice, train, and rehearse at being negative, that's what you will be good at. Negative! However, if you practice, train, and rehearse being spiritually positive, that means you trust the outcome will be for the best. Because simply good or ok is the enemy of the best.

I have experienced the void throughout my spiritual journey. It is my ability to live near the void, go into it at will, and make it my friend that will assist me in growing even faster and with more joy.

Remember, there is nothing going to happen today that you and God cannot handle. It just feels like it. So enjoy the journey. While drafting this book, I was plagued by fear, self-doubt, and unworthiness. I could not use words that discouraged or supported my fears that I was not educated enough and would never draft a book. Instead, I used the carrot-and-stick approach that farmers use to get the mule to pull the wagon by placing a carrot in front of him to get him to move, which in this case would be the joy of completing the book. Or the farmer whips the mule with the stick to get him going. The stick for me would be how I would feel about me not finishing this book.

Spiritual Tools and Mental Health: Techniques for Nurturing Mental Well-being

A spiritual tool is a non-material practice that can be utilized at any given time (when willing) that can promote a change in my attitude, outlook, self-awakening, and quality of life. These action-based tools are not to be used to fix others but to create correction, repair, molding, and mending within me.

CULTIVATING POSITIVE THOUGHTS AND MINDSET

Planting Seeds of Spiritual Growth: Exploring Spiritual Practices for Inner Harmony

In this chapter, we will explore the transformative power of intention-setting and its profound influence on shaping our thoughts, beliefs, and actions. By delving into the practice of setting clear and heartfelt intentions, we discover how they serve as seeds that manifest our desires and shape the direction of our lives.

We create affirmations that resonate with our true desires and values, thus aligning our intentions with our core beliefs. By setting specific, achievable goals that are in harmony with our intentions, we empower ourselves to take focused and purposeful steps toward their realization.

To get started:

1. Clarify your goals or what you want to achieve.
2. Set aside dedicated time for the exercise where you can focus.
3. Write down your intentions clearly and positively, using affirming language.
4. Visualize yourself achieving these intentions to reinforce them.
5. Take action steps aligned with your intentions to manifest them effectively.

Through reflective exercises, storytelling, and actionable tips:

1. Reflect on your priorities: Just like a gardener plans out which plants to prioritize for growth, take time to reflect on your values and priorities. This will help you discern when to say no to activities or requests that do not align with your true path. If you don't know how to say no, you really never said yes.
2. Set boundaries: Like setting up a fence to protect your garden, establish clear boundaries with others. Communicate your limits kindly but firmly, and do not be afraid to say no when something does not feel right for you.
3. Practice mindfulness: Cultivate mindfulness to tune into your intuition and inner guidance. This will help you make decisions from a place of clarity and authenticity, just like a gardener listens to the needs of their plants.
4. Learn to delegate: Just as a gardener enlists the help of others for certain tasks, do not be afraid to delegate or ask for support when needed. Saying no to taking on too much responsibility is essential for maintaining balance and well-being.
5. Celebrate your growth: Finally, remember that saying no is a form of self-care and empowerment. Celebrate each time you honor your boundaries and prioritize your well-being, nurturing your inner garden with love and mindfulness. I aim to inspire readers to harness the creative power of intention-setting, cultivate a positive mindset, and manifest their aspirations with clarity and conviction. We delve into the essential role of self-awareness and mindfulness in nurturing our inner garden of well-being. We explore how developing a deeper understanding of our thoughts, emotions, and patterns can empower us to cultivate a more harmonious and thriving internal landscape.

By discussing various practices that can aid in this cultivation, such as meditation, breathwork, and journaling, these tools enhance our present-moment awareness, foster clarity of mind, and facilitate a deeper connection with our inner selves, a bridge to a higher consciousness.

Through practical insights, firsthand experiences, and guidance on incorporating these practices into daily life, I aim to guide readers on this transformative journey toward greater self-awareness and mindfulness for their mental and spiritual well-being. I cultivate awareness by sharing real-life examples of how these practices have personally impacted my mental well-being and spiritual growth. Readers can integrate mindfulness practices into their daily routines. I cannot emphasize enough the importance of consistency and patience in nurturing self-awareness.

Explore the neuroscience behind mindfulness and self-awareness, highlighting how these practices can rewire the brain, reduce stress, and enhance overall cognitive functioning. Scientific evidence can help readers understand the profound benefits of incorporating these tools into their lives.

Finally, by incorporating reflective exercises or prompts to encourage readers to engage actively with the content and apply the concepts discussed to your own journey of self-discovery and inner cultivation, planting seeds of intention further, I invite you to explore insights on the psychology behind intention-setting and how it influences our subconscious mind to work toward our goals by discussing the concept of visualization as a powerful tool to reinforce our intentions and create a mental blueprint for success. Proverbs 29:18 (KJV) reads, "Where there is no vision, the people perish" (Bible n.d.).

It is important to align our intentions with our values and purpose in life to cultivate a sense of authenticity and fulfillment. Share strategies for overcoming obstacles and limiting beliefs that may hinder the realization of our intentions; emphasize the role of self-compassion and resilience in staying committed to our goals.

I have included personal anecdotes that illustrate the transformative impact of intention-setting in different areas of life, such as relationships, career, and personal growth. These real-life examples can provide inspiration and practical guidance for readers on how to apply intention-setting effectively in their own lives.

Relationships

- Goal: Improve communication with my partner by actively listening and expressing my feelings openly. We can have the same beliefs but different rules on how to practice them. I do not know your rules, so I listen. We both agree if we tell the truth; that is you showing love. However, if it hurts you, I do not tell you. For example, I withhold telling you I broke your favorite cup. I am afraid you will be mad when I tell you, so I don't because of our love rule.
- Intention: Cultivate empathy and understanding in all my relationships by practicing kindness and patience.
- Action steps: Schedule regular check-ins with my partner, attend a couples' communication workshop, and practice active listening techniques.

Career

- Goal: Advance to a leadership position within my company within the next year.
- Intention: Develop my leadership skills and influence within the organization to drive positive change.
- Action steps: Enroll in a leadership development course, seek mentorship from current leaders, and take on additional leadership responsibilities.

Personal Growth

- Goal: Enhance my emotional intelligence and self-awareness to improve overall well-being.
- Intention: Prioritize self-care practices and mindfulness techniques to boost personal growth.
- Action steps: Start a daily meditation practice, journal about emotions and experiences, and attend therapy or coaching sessions for self-discovery.

Setting clear intentions and actionable goals in these areas can help you stay focused, motivated, and aligned with your aspirations.

SEED TO PLANT

Just like a tiny seed is buried in darkness before it can sprout and grow into a vibrant plant, we too may face dark or challenging times that eventually lead to personal growth and new beginnings.

Let us explore the importance of setting boundaries and saying no to what does not align with your true path. Just like a gardener tends to their plants, nurturing your inner garden requires mindful attention and care. Remember, it is okay to prioritize your well-being and protect your energy like a gardener protects their garden from invasive weeds.

Reflective Exercise

Take a few moments to consider a recent situation where you struggled to say no. How did it make you feel? What boundaries could you put in place to honor your needs and values in similar scenarios in the future?

Now, let us delve into the concept of planting seeds of intention. Just as a gardener plants seeds with the intention of growing a thriving garden, setting intentions creates a road map for reaching your goals. Your subconscious mind is like fertile soil ready to nurture these intentions and help them bloom.

Reflective Exercise

Think about a goal you have in mind. How can you formulate a clear and concise intention to support this goal? Consider writing it down and visualizing yourself achieving it to reinforce your commitment.

Visualization is a powerful tool that can supercharge your intentions. By creating a mental blueprint of success, you are priming your mind to work toward your goals with clarity and purpose. Just as a gardener envisions a lush garden before planting seeds, visualize your success to manifest your desired outcomes.

Reflective Exercise

Find a quiet space to sit and visualize yourself accomplishing your goal. What do you see, hear, and feel in this moment of achievement? How can you incorporate this visualization practice into your daily routine to stay connected to your intentions?

By actively engaging with these reflective exercises and incorporating intention-setting and visualization into your daily routine, you are nurturing the seeds of growth within you. Just like a garden flourishing with care and attention, your inner garden will bloom with purpose and fulfillment as you cultivate a mindset of abundance and authenticity.

Feeling Word List

Pleasant Feelings Positive Seeds

OPEN	HAPPY	ALIVE	GOOD
understanding	great	playful	calm
confident	gay	courageous	peaceful
reliable	joyous	energetic	at ease
easy	lucky	liberated	comfortable
amazed	fortunate	optimistic	pleased
free	delighted	provocative	encouraged
sympathetic	overjoyed	impulsive	clever
interested	gleeful	free	surprised
satisfied	thankful	frisky	content
receptive	important	animated	quiet
accepting	festive	spirited	certain
kind	ecstatic	thrilled	relaxed
	satisfied	wonderful	serene
	glad		Free & easy
	cheerful		bright
	sunny		blessed
	merry		reassured
	elated		
	jubilant		

Gardening Your Mind with Spiritual Tools

LOVE	INTERESTED	POSITIVE	STRONG
loving	concerned	eager	impulsive
considerate	affected	keen	free
affectionate	fascinated	earnest	sure
sensitive	intrigued	intent	certain
tender	absorbed	anxious	rebellious
devoted	inquisitive	inspired	unique
attracted	nosy	determined	dynamic
Passionate	snoopy	excited	tenacious
admiration	engrossed	enthusiastic	hardy
warm	curious	bold	secure
touched		brave	
sympathy		daring	
close		challenged	
loved		optimistic	
comforted		reinforced	
drawn toward		confident	
		hopeful	

29

Positive Feeling Words Meaning

Open: receptive or willing to consider new ideas or information

- Understanding: empathetic comprehension of someone's feelings or situation
- Confident: having faith in one's abilities or qualities
- Reliable: able to be trusted or depended on
- Easy: not hard or difficult; requiring little effort
- Amazed: greatly surprised or impressed
- Free: not under the control or in the power of another; able to act or be done as one wishes
- Sympathetic: showing concern for someone else's feelings or well-being
- Interested: showing curiosity or concern about something
- Satisfied: content or pleased with a situation or outcome
- Receptive: willing to consider or accept new suggestions and ideas
- Kind: having a gentle nature; showing compassion and consideration for others

Happy: feeling or showing pleasure or contentment

- Great: of an extent, amount, or intensity considerably above the norm or average
- Gay: lighthearted and carefree
- Joyous: full of happiness and joy
- Lucky: having, bringing, or resulting from good luck
- Fortunate: favored by or involving good luck or fortune
- Delighted: feeling or showing great pleasure
- Overjoyed: extremely happy or joyful
- Gleeful: full of exuberant joy or delight
- Thankful: feeling or expressing gratitude
- Important: significant or of great significance
- Festive: relating to a celebration or festival
- Ecstatic: feeling or expressing overwhelming happiness or joyful excitement
- Satisfied: content or pleased with a situation or outcome

- Glad: pleased; happy
- Cheerful: noticeably happy and optimistic
- Sunny: bright, full of light, or characterized by happiness
- Merry: cheerful and full of festive spirit
- Elated: extremely happy and excited
- Jubilant: feeling or expressing great happiness and triumph-

Alive: living or having life

- Playful: full of fun and playfulness
- Courageous: possessing or showing bravery in the face of fear or danger
- Energetic: possessing or showing vigor, enthusiasm, or liveliness
- Liberated: feeling free from constraints or limitations
- Optimistic: hopeful and confident about the future
- Provocative: causing anger, annoyance, or another strong reaction, especially deliberately
- Impulsive: acting or done without forethought
- Free: not under the control or in the power of another; able to act or be done as one wishes
- Frisky: lively, playful, and full of energy
- Animated: full of life or excitement
- Spirited: full of energy, enthusiasm, or determination
- Thrilled: experiencing a sudden feeling of excitement or pleasure
- Wonderful: extremely good; marvelous or great

Good: satisfactory in quality, quantity, or degree

- Calm: not showing or feeling nervousness, anger, or other strong emotions
- Peaceful: free from disturbance; tranquil
- At ease: feeling relaxed and comfortable
- Comfortable: providing physical ease and relaxation
- Pleased: feeling satisfaction or joy
- Encourage: give support, confidence, or hope to someone
- Clever: quick to understand, learn, and devise new skills or ideas
- Surprise: cause someone to feel mild astonishment or shock by doing or saying something unexpected

- Content: in a state of peaceful happiness
- Certain: knowing something for sure; free from doubt
- Relax: make or become less tense or anxious
- Serene: calm, peaceful, and untroubled
- Free and easy: relaxed, casual, and informal
- Bright: giving out or reflecting a lot of light; shining
- Blessed: endowed with divine favor and protection
- Reassure: say or do something to remove the doubts or fears of someone

Love: a strong feeling of affection and care toward someone

- Loving: feeling or showing love and affection
- Considerate: careful not to cause inconvenience or hurt to others
- Affectionate: showing fondness or tenderness towards someone
- Sensitive: aware of and responsive to the feelings of others
- Tender: showing gentleness, kindness, and affection
- Devoted: showing loyalty and support
- Attracted: feeling drawn to someone or something
- Passionate: showing or expressing strong emotions or beliefs
- Admiration: a feeling of respect and approval
- Warm: friendly, kind, or giving a feeling of comfort
- Touched: emotionally moved or affected
- Sympathetic: showing concern for someone's feelings or situation
- Close: having a strong emotional bond or connection
- Comforted: feeling relieved or reassured
- Drawn toward: feeling an attraction or inclination toward someone or something

Interested: feeling or showing curiosity or concern about something

- Concern: feeling of worry or interest in something important
- Affected: influenced or touched by an external factor or feeling
- Fascinated: extremely interested or attracted
- Intrigued: curious or interested about something in a mysterious way
- Absorbed: completely engrossed or involved in something

- Inquisitive: showing curiosity; eager to learn or investigate
- Nosy: excessively inquisitive or curious about other people's affairs
- Snoopy: overly curious or prying
- Grossed curious: having a strong desire to know or learn something

Positive: characterized by the presence of features or qualities rather than their absence

- Eager: keen or enthusiastic
- Key: extremely important or significant
- Earnest: showing sincere and intense conviction
- Intent: purpose or plan
- Anxious: feeling or showing worry or unease about something with an uncertain outcome
- Inspired: filled with the urge or ability to do or feel something creative
- Determined: having a strong desire and motivation to achieve a goal
- Excited: feeling eager and enthusiastic
- Enthusiastic: showing intense enjoyment, interest, or approval
- Bold: showing willingness to take risks; confident and courageous
- Brave: ready to face and endure danger or pain
- Daring: willing to take risks; adventurous or bold
- Challenged: feeling energized or motivated by a difficult task or goal
- Optimistic: hopeful and confident about the future
- Reinforce: strengthen or support
- Confident: feeling sure about one's own abilities or qualities
- Hopeful: feeling or inspiring optimism about a future outcome-

Strong: having the power to move heavy weights or perform other physically demanding tasks

- Impulsive: acting or done without forethought
- Free: not under the control or in the power of another; able to act or be done as one wishes
- Sure: confident in what one thinks or knows

- Certain: known for sure; established beyond doubt
- Rebellious: resisting control or authority; defying rules or norms
- Unique: being the only one of its kind; unlike anything else
- Dynamic: characterized by constant change, activity, or progress
- Tenacious: determined and persistent in holding onto or achieving something
- Hardy: robust and capable of enduring difficult conditions
- Secure: feeling safe, stable, and free from danger

Afraid: feeling fear or unease

- Fearless: lacking fear; brave or bold
- Terrified: extremely frightened
- Suspicious: having or showing a cautious distrust of someone or something
- Anxiety: a feeling of worry, nervousness, or unease about something with an uncertain outcome
- Alarmed: feeling sudden fear or distress
- Panic: a sudden uncontrollable fear or anxiety
- Nervous: easily agitated or worried
- Scared: feeling fear or fright
- Worried: anxious or troubled about actual or potential problems
- Timid: showing a lack of courage or confidence; easily frightened
- Shaky: trembling or unsteady, often due to fear or nervousness
- Restless: unable to relax or rest, often due to anxiety or impatience
- Doubtful: feeling uncertain or lacking conviction
- Threaten: to express an intention to harm or cause problems for someone or something
- Cowardly: lacking courage or bravery
- Quaking: trembling or shaking, often due to fear
- Menace: a person or thing that is likely to cause harm; a threat
- Wary: feeling or showing caution about possible dangers or problems

EMBRACING SELF-LOVE AND DISCERNMENT

Tools Needed

- **Gardening gloves** represent the protective measures you take while nurturing your growth. Just as gloves protect your hands from rough edges and thorns, self-love involves setting healthy boundaries to protect yourself from negativity and harm while you grow and evolve.
- **Rake** symbolizes the practice of gathering and organizing your values, priorities, and emotions. Just as a rake gathers leaves and debris, helping to keep the garden clean, you need to regularly sort through your thoughts and feelings to maintain clarity and focus on what truly matters to you.
- **Sunlight** represents the essential need for self-care and maintaining a positive environment. Just like plants need sunlight to grow, your well-being thrives when you expose yourself to positive influences, practice self-compassion, and take time for activities that bring you joy and fulfillment.

In our journey toward self-love, we must first acknowledge and confront the negative beliefs that have been ingrained in us, the idea of unworthiness. It is vital to recognize that it is not shameful to embrace our true selves authentically.

Learning to love ourselves starts with meeting our own needs and understanding that self-care is not selfish but necessary for our well-being. As we pave this path of self-discovery, we begin to shed the layers of self-doubt and insecurity that cloud our perception of worthiness.

However, embracing self-love is not solely about unconditional acceptance but also about practicing discernment. By honing our ability to discern what serves our highest good and what does not, we empower ourselves to make choices aligned with our values and aspirations.

In this chapter, we delve into the intertwined journey of self-love and discernment, exploring how these two pillars support our quest for inner peace and fulfillment. Through introspection and self-awareness, we pave the way for a more profound connection with ourselves and cultivate a foundation of love and acceptance that radiates into every aspect of our lives. First, let us remove some of the weeds to clear the ground (our mind) a bit to make room for seeds of self-attention, self-affection, self-approval, and self-acceptance.

Today, I Make Space for Miracles

"I realize that the significance of a miracle is not its size, but rather the extent of space I can open up for it."

The sponsee went to see his sponsor, asking for advice on becoming sober and living a spiritual life. The sponsee, brimming with thoughts and opinions, barely listened as he incessantly talked about what he had tried, what he believed, and what he thought should work. He interrupted the sponsor repeatedly with his own stories and failed to listen to what the sponsor had to say.

The sponsor patiently listened for a while and then handed the sponsee a cup and began to pour tea. The sponsee watched as the cup filled and then began to overflow, spilling tea onto the table.

"Stop! The cup is full. No more will go in!" exclaimed the sponsee.

The sponsor replied, "Like this cup, you are full of your own ideas and opinions. You cannot learn until you first empty your cup. Come back to me with an empty cup."

The story of the sponsee with the overflowing cup can be beautifully paralleled with the concept of *Gardening Your Mind with Spiritual Tools*. In the narrative, the sponsee symbolizes a person whose mind is so full of their own opinions, knowledge, and preconceived notions that there is no space to truly listen, learn, and grow. Similarly, in the process of gardening our minds, we are challenged to acknowledge and prune away the overgrowth of limiting beliefs, self-criticism, and closed-mindedness that prevent us from experiencing personal transformation and spiritual growth.

Just as the sponsor poured tea into the overflowing cup to demonstrate the sponsee's closed-mindedness, the practice of *Gardening Your Mind with Spiritual Tools* invites us to reflect on our own tendencies to fill our mental and spiritual spaces with clutter and noise. By recognizing when our cups are overflowing with rigidity, doubts, or negativity, we can learn to empty ourselves of these obstacles and create room for fresh perspectives, self-compassion, and spiritual renewal. The wisdom of the sponsor's gentle yet powerful gesture serves as a reminder that only by approaching life with an open and empty cup—free from the burdens of the past and the constraints of the ego—can we truly receive the richness of new insights, growth, and inner peace.

INNER GROWTH AND TRANSFORMATION

Weeding Out Negativity

Tools Needed

- **Seed packets** represent innovative ideas, habits, or goals that you plant in your mind. Just as seeds contain the potential for growth, introducing new positive thoughts and practices into your daily routine can lead to significant personal transformation over time.
- **Garden hose** symbolizes the steady stream of resources, support, and ongoing effort needed to nurture your growth. Just as a garden hose provides water to sustain plants, consistent self-care, learning, and support from others are crucial for fostering inner growth.
- **Mulch** represents the protective and enriching practices that support your mental and emotional growth. Mulch helps retain moisture and prevents weeds, symbolizing the need to protect your mind from negativity while nourishing it with positive affirmations, mindfulness practices, and beneficial habits.

Overcoming obstacles keeps you in a loop of negative thoughts, constantly replaying past events or worrying about the future. This constant replaying of negative thoughts can lead to excessive worry, anxiety, and stress. Just like a snowball rolling down a hill, your worries and fears can grow bigger and more overwhelming the more you dwell on them. Your mind becomes consumed by these negative thoughts, making it hard to focus on anything else or find peace.

In terms of spiritual growth and emotional health, rumination can act like a dark cloud blocking the sunshine. It hinders your ability to connect with your inner self, find peace, and experience personal growth. Instead of moving forward and evolving, you get trapped in this cycle of negativity that weighs you down and blurs your path to spiritual fulfillment.

Breaking free from rumination is like opening a window to let fresh air in. By recognizing and challenging these repetitive negative thoughts, you can create space for growth, inner peace, and a healthier emotional state. It is about stepping out of the cycle of worry and stress to nurture your spiritual well-being and emotional health and challenges.

Understanding Rumination

Explore what rumination is and how it differs from reflection or contemplation. Delve into the cyclical nature of rumination and its impact on mental well-being.

Recognizing Negative Patterns

I will discuss how rumination can lead to excessive worry, anxiety, and stress. I will highlight the detrimental effects of repetitive negative thinking on spiritual growth and emotional health. Imagine your mind is like a broken record that keeps playing the same sad song over and over again. This repetitive thinking pattern is what we call *rumination*. When you ruminate, you get stuck in a loop of negative thoughts, constantly replaying past events or worrying about the future.

This constant replaying of negative thoughts can lead to excessive worry, anxiety, and stress. Just like a snowball rolling down a hill, your worries and fears can grow bigger and more overwhelming the more you dwell on them.

Your mind becomes consumed by these negative thoughts, making it hard to focus on anything else or find peace.

In terms of spiritual growth and emotional health, rumination can act like a dark cloud blocking the sunshine. It hinders your ability to connect with your inner self, find peace, and experience personal growth. Instead of moving forward and evolving, you get trapped in this cycle of negativity that weighs you down and blurs your path to spiritual fulfillment.

Breaking free from rumination is like opening a window to let in fresh air. By recognizing and challenging these repetitive negative thoughts, you can create space for growth, inner peace, and a healthier emotional state. It is about stepping out of the cycle of worry and stress to nurture your spiritual well-being and emotional health.

What makes rumination a form of psychological injury is that it does not provide any new understanding that could heal our wounds; instead it serves only to pick at our scabs and infect them anew.

Unfortunately, our tendency to ruminate is set off almost solely by painful feelings and experiences and rarely by positive or joyful ones (Winch 2014).

Resolving Day-to-Day Issues

Running away from any problem only increases the distance from the solution. The easiest way to escape from the problem is to solve it.

The following spiritual terms involve approaching challenges from a perspective that integrates spiritual principles and practices. Here are some steps to help explain this concept:

1. Mindfulness is being present in the moment and practicing awareness of thoughts and emotions when facing daily issues, regardless of how painful it is to stay present and not be unconscious.
2. Self-reflection is looking within to understand the root causes of challenges and using introspection for personal growth. For

example, "Feel my feelings and do not let them destroy me or pretend I am not having them."
3. Compassion is approaching problems with empathy and kindness toward oneself and others, fostering understanding and resolution. For example, "Stop shaming myself and others about being human."
4. Gratitude is the practice of finding gratitude in demanding situations, shifting perspectives, and promoting a positive mindset, knowing it could be worse.
5. Intuition is listening to inner guidance or intuition when making decisions and tapping into spiritual wisdom for problem-solving. It is being led in a positive direction without proof of the outcome.

By incorporating these spiritual aspects into the process of addressing day-to-day issues, individuals can cultivate resilience, inner peace, and a deeper connection to God, themselves, and the world around them. Do you have a personalized guide to apply spiritual principles to resolve day-to-day challenges?

I have outlined a personalized approach to resolving day-to-day issues in spiritual terms. Consider the following:

1. Daily practices: Implement a daily spiritual practice such as meditation, journaling, or prayer to center yourself and gain clarity when facing challenges.
2. Guided reflection: Use reflective questions or prompts to delve deeper into the spiritual lessons and growth opportunities presented by daily obstacles.
3. Seek support: Connect with a spiritual community, mentor, or guide who can offer insights and support as you navigate day-to-day issues from a spiritual perspective.
4. Visualization: Use visualization techniques to imagine positive outcomes and align your energy with solutions rooted in spiritual principles.
5. Manifestation: Practice manifesting intentions through affirmations, visualizations, or rituals that align with your spiritual beliefs to address and overcome daily challenges.

By incorporating these personalized approaches, I have cultivated a deeper spiritual connection and resilience to effectively navigate and resolve day-to-day issues.

A life under new management with a spiritual perspective involves embracing the idea of surrendering control to a higher power, inner wisdom, or spiritual guidance. Here are some key points to consider when this transformation happens.

- Surrender and Trust: I encourage letting go of the need to control every aspect of life and cultivating trust in a higher power or spiritual guidance to manage outcomes.
- Alignment with Values: Align life decisions and actions with spiritual principles, values, beliefs, and rules to create a sense of purpose and meaning.
- Mindfulness and Presence: I advocate for living in the present moment, practicing mindfulness, and being aware of the spiritual significance in everyday experiences.
- Gratitude and Acceptance: While promoting an attitude of gratitude for the present moment and acceptance of life's challenges, view them as opportunities for growth and learning.
- Service and Contribution: The final and most important piece is serving others, contributing to the greater good, and finding fulfillment through selfless acts guided by spiritual principles.

By integrating these elements into a life under new management, individuals can experience a deeper connection to their spiritual path, a sense of inner peace, and a greater alignment with their higher purpose.

I cannot emphasize enough the importance of finding a balance between reflecting on spiritual matters and taking actionable steps toward growth and transformation, guiding you through integrating contemplation into practical spirituality.

Balancing reflection and action in matters of spirituality involves harmonizing introspection with tangible steps toward personal growth and transformation. Here is how you can integrate contemplation into practical spirituality:

Reflection on Spiritual Matters

- Purpose: Take time to reflect on your beliefs, values, and connection to the divine or higher purpose.
- Practice: Engage in meditation, prayer, journaling, or spiritual reading to deepen your understanding and connection with the spiritual realm.

Taking Actual Steps Toward Growth

- Purpose: Translate insights from reflection into actions that promote spiritual growth and transformation in daily life.
- Practice: Act on your values by practicing kindness, compassion, forgiveness, and service to others. Set goals aligned with your spiritual principles and take concrete steps to achieve them.

Integrating Reflection and Action

- Purpose: Fuse introspective contemplation with practical application to cultivate a holistic and authentic spiritual practice.
- Practice: Reflect on spiritual teachings or experiences, identify key insights, and actively integrate these lessons into your thoughts, words, and deeds.

By striking a balance between reflection and action in your spiritual journey, you can deepen your understanding, align your beliefs with your behaviors, and experience meaningful growth and transformation. It is about harmonizing inner contemplation with outward expression, integrating the wisdom gained from reflection into practical spirituality that positively impacts your life and the lives of those around you.

ACCEPTANCE AND SURRENDER

Tools Needed

- **Wheelbarrow** represents the ability to carry and manage the emotional load that comes with acceptance and surrender. Just as a wheelbarrow helps you transport heavy materials in the garden, developing emotional resilience and coping strategies can help you manage the weight of challenging experiences and emotions.
- **Rain** symbolizes the natural flow of life and the necessity to embrace and go with it. Just as rain nourishes plants and is an unavoidable part of nature, learning to accept and surrender to life's ups and downs allows for growth and nurtures a more peaceful state of mind.
- **Garden stakes** represent the support and stability needed during times of vulnerability and change. Just as garden stakes support growing plants that might otherwise bend or break, cultivating a support system of friends, family, or mentors can help you stay grounded and resilient as you navigate acceptance and surrender.

Let's explore themes of acceptance, letting go, and surrendering control in the context of rumination by trusting in the spiritual journey and releasing excessive mental burdens.

Overall, the chapter on rumination could offer a holistic perspective on how to cultivate a healthy and productive mindset using spiritual tools within the framework of gardening your mind for spiritual growth and your well-being.

Embracing acceptance and surrender in the context of rumination involves letting go of the need to control every thought or outcome and trusting in your spiritual journey. By releasing the grip of excessive mental burden, you can find peace and freedom from the cycle of rumination.

Here is how you can practice acceptance and surrender to trust your spiritual path:

- Acceptance: Acknowledge and accept the presence of negative thoughts and emotions without judgment or resistance. Understand that it's normal to have worries and fears but you don't have to be defined by them. Practice self-compassion and forgiveness toward yourself for not being able to control every thought.
- Surrender: Let go of the need to constantly analyze or fixate on negative thoughts, allowing them to pass without attaching significance. Trust in God or a higher power, universal wisdom, or the flow of life to guide you on your spiritual journey. Surrender the illusion of control and embrace the beauty of uncertainty and growth that comes with trusting in the process.
- Releasing excessive mental burden: Release the mental burden of trying to control every outcome or thought, freeing up mental and emotional space for peace and clarity. Cultivate a mindset of surrendering what you cannot change and focusing on what you can influence positively. Practice mindfulness and being present in the moment, allowing yourself to let go of worries about the past or future.

By embracing acceptance and surrender, you can release the weight of the excessive mental burden caused by rumination, allowing trust in your spiritual journey to flourish. It is about relinquishing the need for absolute control, finding peace in uncertainty, and opening yourself to the transformative power of surrendering to the flow of life. Say several times through the day the Serenity Prayer, "God/Higher Power/Great Spirit/Who or What you Believe In, grant me the serenity to accept the things I cannot change, the courage to change the things I can, and the wisdom to know the difference. Amen."

> "Wear the world like a loose garment, which touches
> us in a few places and there lightly."
> St. Francis of Assisi

EMBRACING COURAGE AND RESILIENCE

When I encounter painful experiences, I typically reflect on them, hoping to reach the kinds of insights and epiphanies that reduce my distress and allow me to move on. For many of us who engage in this process of self-reflection, things go awry. Instead of attaining an emotional release, we get caught in a vicious cycle of rumination in which we replay the same distressing scenes, memories, and feelings repeatedly, feeling worse every time we do. We become like hamsters trapped in a wheel of emotional pain, running endlessly but going nowhere.

What makes rumination a form of psychological injury is that it provides no new understanding that could heal our wounds and instead serves only to pick at our scabs and infect them anew (Winch 2014).

Unfortunately, our tendency to ruminate is set off solely by painful feelings and experiences and rarely by positive or joyful ones. Pruning fearful branches in our lives involves facing painful experiences with courage and resilience to find insight and epiphanies that reduce distress and enable us to move forward. Here is how you can embrace courage and resilience in the face of challenging circumstances:

Courage

- Facing fear: Confronting challenging or fearful situations with bravery and determination rather than avoiding or denying them

- Vulnerability: Allowing yourself to be vulnerable and open to the possibility of discomfort in order to grow and heal
- Taking action: Making conscious choices to move forward despite uncertainty or fear, trusting in your inner strength and resilience

Resilience

- Adaptability: Being flexible and adaptive in response to adversity, bouncing back from setbacks, and learning from difficult experiences
- Positive outlook: Cultivating a mindset of optimism and perseverance, seeing challenges as opportunities for growth and transformation
- Self-care: Prioritizing self-care practices that nurture your emotional well-being and build resilience in the face of adversity

Seeking Insight and Epiphanies

- Reflection: Taking time to reflect on painful experiences, seeking deeper understanding and meaning to gain insights that facilitate healing
- Learning: Embracing painful experiences as opportunities for learning and growth, allowing them to be catalysts for positive change in your life
- Embracing transformation: Using epiphanies and insights gained from challenging moments to cultivate personal transformation and resilience

By pruning fearful branches through courage and resilience, you can navigate painful experiences with strength and grace, seeking insights and epiphanies that lead to healing and growth. It is about embracing the journey of self-discovery and empowerment, using challenging moments as stepping stones toward a more resilient and fulfilling life.

Difficult/Unpleasant Feelings Weeds

ANGRY	DEPRESSED	CONFUSED	HELPLESS
irritated	lousy	upset	incapable
enraged	disappointed	doubtful	alone
hostile	discouraged	uncertain	paralyzed
insulting	ashamed	indecisive	fatigued
sore	powerless	perplexed	useless
annoyed	diminished	embarrassed	inferior
upset	guilty	hesitant	vulnerable
hateful	dissatisfied	shy	empty
unpleasant	miserable	stupefied	forced
offensive	detestable	disillusioned	hesitant
bitter	repugnant	unbelieving	Despair
aggressive	despicable	skeptical	frustrated
resentful	disgusting	distrustful	distressed
inflamed	abominable	misgiving	woeful
provoked	terrible	lost	pathetic
incensed	in despair	unsure	tragic
infuriated	sulky	uneasy	in a stew
cross	bad	pessimistic	dominated
worked up	sense of loss	tense	
boiling			
fuming			
indignant			

INDIFFERENT	AFRAID	HURT	SAD
insensitive	fearful	crushed	tearful
dull	terrified	tormented	sorrowful
nonchalant	suspicious	deprived	pained
neutral	anxious	pained	grief
reserved	alarmed	tortured	anguish
weary	panic	dejected	desolate
bored	nervous	rejected	desperate
preoccupied	scared	injured	pessimistic
cold	worried	offended	unhappy

disinterested	frightened	afflicted	lonely
lifeless	timid	aching	grieved
	shaky	victimized	mournful
restless	heartbroken	dismayed	
doubtful	agonized		
threatened	appalled		
cowardly	humiliated		
quaking	wronged		
menaced	alienated		
wary			

Negative Feeling Words Meaning

Afraid: feeling fear or unease

- Fearless: lacking fear; brave or bold
- Terrified: extremely frightened
- Suspicious: having or showing a cautious distrust of someone or something
- Anxiety: a feeling of worry, nervousness, or unease about something with an uncertain outcome
- Alarmed: feeling sudden fear or distress
- Panic: a sudden uncontrollable fear or anxiety
- Nervous: easily agitated or worried
- Scared: feeling fear or fright
- Worried: anxious or troubled about actual or potential problems
- Timid: showing a lack of courage or confidence; easily frightened
- Shaky: trembling or unsteady, often due to fear or nervousness
- Restless: unable to relax or rest, often due to anxiety or impatience
- Doubtful: feeling uncertain or lacking conviction
- Threaten: to express an intention to harm or cause problems for someone or something
- Cowardly: lacking courage or bravery
- Quaking: trembling or shaking, often due to fear
- Menace: a person or thing likely to cause harm; a threat

- Wary: feeling or showing caution about possible dangers or problems
- Anxiety: a feeling of worry, nervousness, or unease about something with an uncertain outcome
- Alarmed: feeling sudden fear or distress
- Panic: a sudden uncontrollable fear or anxiety
- Nervous: easily agitated or worried
- Scared: feeling fear or fright
- Worried: anxious or troubled about actual or potential problems
- Timid: showing a lack of courage or confidence; easily frightened
- Shaky: trembling or unsteady, often due to fear or nervousness
- Restless: unable to relax or rest, often due to anxiety or impatience
- Doubtful: feeling uncertain or lacking conviction
- Threaten: to express an intention to harm or cause problems for someone or something
- Cowardly: lacking courage or bravery
- Quaking: trembling or shaking, often due to fear
- Menace: a person or thing that is likely to cause harm; a threat
- Wary: feeling or showing caution about possible dangers or problems

Hurt: to cause pain or injury to someone

- Crushed: emotionally or mentally devastated or overwhelmed
- Torment: severe physical or mental suffering
- Deprived: lacking the necessities of life; disadvantaged
- Pain: a distressing feeling often caused by intense or damaging stimuli
- Tortured: subjected to severe physical or mental suffering
- Dejected: low in spirits; sad or depressed
- Rejected: dismissed or refused acceptance
- Injured: harmed physically or mentally
- Offended: resentful or upset about something perceived as insulting or unjust
- Afflicted: suffering or experiencing something unpleasant
- Aching: experiencing a continuous, prolonged dull pain
- Victimized: treated unfairly or harmed by others

- Heartbroken: overwhelmed by grief or sadness, especially due to a loss or betrayal
- Agonized: suffering great physical or mental pain
- Appalled: horrified or shocked by something unpleasant or wrong
- Humiliated: made to feel ashamed or foolish
- Wronged: treated unfairly or unjustly
- Alienated: feeling isolated or estranged from others

Sad: feeling unhappy or sorrowful

- Tearful: inclined to or causing tears; weepy
- Sorrowful: full of sadness or distress
- Pain: a distressing feeling often caused by intense or damaging stimuli
- Grief: deep sorrow, especially caused by someone's death
- Anguish: severe mental or physical pain or distress
- Desolate: feeling or showing great unhappiness or loneliness
- Desperate: feeling or showing a hopeless sense that a situation is so bad as to be impossible to deal with
- Pessimistic: tending to see the worst aspect of things or believe that the worst will happen
- Unhappy: not feeling or showing joy or satisfaction
- Lonely: feeling alone or isolated
- Mournful: feeling or expressing sorrow or grief
- Dismay: consternation and distress caused by something unexpected

Depressed: in a state of general unhappiness or despondency

- Lousy: very poor or bad
- Disappointed: feeling let down or disillusioned
- Discouraged: having lost confidence or enthusiasm
- Ashamed: embarrassed or guilty because of one's actions or characteristics
- Powerless: lacking power or strength; helpless
- Diminish: to make or become less

- Guilty: feeling responsible for a wrongdoing or offense
- Dissatisfied: not content or pleased with something
- Miserable: extremely unhappy or uncomfortable
- Detestable: deserving intense dislike; abhorrent
- Repugnant: extremely distasteful or unacceptable
- Disgusting: causing disgust or revulsion

Confused: unable to think clearly or understand

- Upset: disturbed, distressed, or agitated
- Doubtful: feeling uncertain about something
- Uncertain: not able to be relied on; not known or definite
- Indecisive: unable to make a decision
- Perplexed: completely baffled or puzzled
- Embarrassed: feeling self-conscious or ashamed
- Hesitant: tentative or unsure
- Shy: being reserved or showing nervousness or timidity in the company of others
- Stupefied: shocked or stunned into silence or inaction
- Disillusion: to disappoint someone by breaking their belief in a false idea
- Unbelieving: skeptical or unwilling to believe
- Skeptical: doubtful about a particular thing
- Distrustful: lacking trust or confidence in something or someone

Helpless: unable to defend oneself or to act without help

- Incapable: unable to do something effectively
- Alone: by oneself; solitary
- Paralyzed: incapable of movement
- Fatigued: exhausted or worn out
- Useless: not fulfilling or not expected to achieve the intended purpose or desired outcome
- Inferior: lower in rank, status, or quality
- Vulnerable: susceptible to physical or emotional harm
- Empty: lacking meaning or substance; vacant

- Force: strength or energy as an attribute of physical action or movement
- Hesitant: tentative or unsure
- Despair: the complete loss or absence of hope
- Frustrated: feeling or expressing distress and annoyance resulting from an inability to change or achieve something
- Distressed: suffering from extreme anxiety, sorrow, or pain
- Woeful: full of sorrow or distress
- Pathetic: arousing pity, especially through vulnerability or sadness
- Tragic: causing or characterized by extreme distress or sorrow
- Dominated: controlled or governed by something or someone else

LEARNING TO LOVE

Tools Needed

- **Flower seeds** represent the potential for love and relationships to blossom. Just as flower seeds have the potential to grow into beautiful blooms with the right conditions, you have the inherent potential to cultivate and nurture love in your life through openness, care, and commitment.
- **Fertilizer** symbolizes the nurturing and enriching practices that enhance your capacity to love. Just as fertilizer provides essential nutrients that help plants thrive, healthy self-care practices, emotional growth, and positive affirmations can enrich your ability to give and receive love.
- **Garden pathway** represents creating a clear and mindful way toward loving relationships. Just as a pathway directs you through a garden, intentional actions and mindful practices can help you navigate the complexities of building and maintaining loving relationships, ensuring that your journey is thoughtful and purposeful.

I could not learn to love myself enough to meet my own needs until I started to release the old attitudes and feelings that I was unworthy, somehow shameful to be myself. I could not learn to love myself without learning discernment.

I learned to trust and love myself through learning to make healthier choices about who to trust and what to believe. I could begin to be able to recognize truth through the distortions, false beliefs, and lies. By doing my emotional healing, by changing the dysfunctional attitudes, I started being responsible in my life. That is, I began to have the ability to respond to life honestly in the moment and stop setting myself up to be victimized by untrustworthy people.

The black-and-white thinking of codependence causes me to need others to tell me who I am. Discernment means the ability to decide between right and wrong or to make good judgments and choices. It involves being able to understand and judge situations or people wisely, especially in tricky or unclear circumstances. I had to learn to trust and love myself by learning to make healthier choices about who to trust and what to believe. I began to be able to recognize the truth and throw out the distortions, false beliefs, and lies. By doing my emotional healing, by changing the dysfunctional attitudes, I started being responsible in my life. That is, I began to have the ability to respond to life honestly in the moment.

Until I heal my wounds, until I become honest and clear in my emotional process, I'm not able to be discerning. I'm not capable of responding to life in the now. I'm only able to react out of old grief, out of old tapes. Emotional dependency refers to relying heavily on someone else for my own happiness, self-worth, and emotional well-being. It involves feeling like I need another person to feel complete or validated, leading to an unhealthy attachment and inability to function independently. It is based upon not trusting myself.

HARVESTING INNER PEACE

Tools Needed

- **Harvest basket** represents gathering and appreciating the fruits of your inner work and mindfulness practices. Just as a harvest basket is used to collect ripe produce, regularly reflecting on and acknowledging your progress and the moments of peace you have cultivated can help reinforce and sustain your inner tranquility.
- **Scythe** symbolizes the need to cut away stress and distractions that hinder inner peace. Just as a scythe is used to clear overgrowth, you can practice techniques such as meditation, mindfulness, and setting boundaries to remove sources of stress and mental clutter from your life, allowing more space for peace.
- **Wind chimes** represent the creation of a serene and calming environment. Wind chimes produce gentle, soothing sounds that promote relaxation and harmony. Similarly, creating a peaceful physical and mental environment through practices like decluttering, listening to calming music, or spending time in nature can enhance your inner peace.

Connecting with Nature and Spirituality

Embrace the fruits of your spiritual and mental labor. Most people have a sense that they are spiritual in some way. You probably feel another worldliness about this universe and the planet you live on. You may sense something far greater and more expansive beyond your comprehension, which drives the universe. You may be religious in your beliefs and behavior by following religious doctrine. Or you may not follow religion at all. You may simply feel a sense of awe about and hold reverence for the universe we live in. You may believe in and try to connect with a godlike being, an ultimate source, a superpower, or an overriding spirit that resides on a higher plane.

You may believe this presence is almighty, all-knowing, all-powerful, indestructible, and infinite. Spirituality is highly individualized. Our spiritual attributes may be very private and confidential. It may be difficult to articulate your spirit because you experience it on a nonverbal or emotional level.

Or you may feel wonderfully comfortable speaking about it publicly or with others you trust. You may encounter your spiritual side through sensations or perceptions that inform you that there is a higher being or greater good, a higher order or presence, a higher meaning or purpose in the universe for humans to connect with and decipher. At times, your spiritual sense may be vague and evasive. It may take your interpretation to understand your inner spiritual inclinations and feelings. You may believe that the source comes from within. On the other hand, you might also understand it as being out there, perceiving it as nature. Or you may refer to it as faith.

You might experience these spiritual beings as highly pleasurable and comforting. At times, you may feel it is judgmental and critical. You may love and be comforted by it. However, at times, you may fear and agonize about it. You may find yourself vacillating between any combination of these beliefs and experiences. Our spirit seems to gravitate toward beliefs in some form or another, be it simple or complex. You may claim there is a large, all-encompassing spirit that is tangible and can be personally known and communicated with. Or you might believe that a holy spirit is neutral, distant, unreachable, unpredictable, unknowable, and mysterious. If you take this stance, then you must infer or interpret your own spiritual beliefs. All of us face uncertainty and the unknown. You came into life without an explanation for why you are here. Other than the drive to survive, we are not pre-programmed with a known purpose.

You must discover meaning and purpose during your lifetime. So as a human, you attempt to make meaning out of your life and the universe. You strive to understand and explain it to yourself. You may turn to people and institutions that present you with explanations and worldviews. You may choose to adopt their ideas. Or you may constantly find yourself trying to understand it all and explain the mystery to yourself.

Harvesting Inner Peace Through Gratitude, Forgiveness, and Letting Go

Tools Needed

- Gratitude journaling: Keeping a journal that lists daily things you are grateful for helps shift focus to positive aspects of life and cultivates a habit of appreciation.
- Forgiveness meditation: Practicing guided meditations specifically aimed at letting go of grudges and forgiving oneself and others can promote emotional healing and inner peace.
- Mindfulness practices: Techniques such as mindful breathing, body scans, and mindful observation help ground individuals in the present moment, aiding in the release of past negative experiences.
- Affirmations: Using positive affirmations related to self-worth, forgiveness, and peace can reprogram the mind to align with these principles, fostering a forgiving and grateful mindset.
- Letting go rituals: Engaging in symbolic activities, such as writing down burdens or regrets and then safely burning the paper, can offer a physical and emotional release, signifying letting go.
- Gratitude visualization: Visualizing moments of gratitude and the impact they've had can reinforce a sense of appreciation and the benefits it brings to one's spiritual and mental state.

- **Pruning shears** represent letting go of what no longer serves us, trimming away habits or thoughts that hinder our spiritual progress.
- **Leaf rake** symbolizes gathering and releasing what is no longer needed in our spiritual journey, making space for new growth.

- **Wheelbarrow** signifies carrying the burdens of our spiritual transformation with grace and strength, moving forward with purpose.
- **Garden gloves** symbolize protection and resilience in our spiritual work, shielding us from harm as we tend to our inner garden.
- **Garden cart** symbolizes the journey of gathering wisdom and experiences on our spiritual path, carrying them forward to nurture our inner landscape.
- **Sun hat** represents the protection and guidance we seek from higher sources during our spiritual journey, shielding us from harmful influences.
- **Reflective garden sphere** represents the act of self-reflection and introspection in our spiritual journey, gaining clarity and insight through contemplation.
- **Garden sanctuary** symbolizes creating a sacred space for inner reflection and meditation, cultivating peace and tranquility within.
- **Zen garden sand rake** signifies the practice of mindfulness and focus on our spiritual work, creating patterns of serenity and balance in the mind.

We continue the journey to explore the profound and transformative effects of gratitude, forgiveness, and letting go in cultivating inner peace and spiritual fulfillment. We delve into the power of these practices in releasing negative energy, fostering emotional healing, and nurturing a sense of harmony within.

It is important to embrace the present moment and find joy in simple everyday experiences, in discovering how mindfulness and gratitude can shift our perspective and elevate our overall well-being. Strategies for cultivating a mindset of abundance and appreciation for the blessings in our lives are shared to guide readers toward a state of inner peace and contentment.

We also address the liberating practice of forgiveness and the art of letting go of past grievances and attachments that weigh us down. By offering techniques for releasing emotional baggage, embracing a mindset of compassion and understanding, we empower readers to free themselves from emotional burdens and find peace within.

Through meditative practices, reflective exercises, and guidance on connecting with the divine or higher self, this chapter aims to inspire readers to harvest inner peace, cultivate a sense of serenity, and embrace a life filled with gratitude, forgiveness, and joy. If the way you're living does not bring you some joy, change the way you're living.

Harvesting the Fruits of Your Inner Garden: Personal Growth and Fulfillment

To further enrich the chapter on harvesting inner peace, consider exploring the psychological and physiological benefits of practices such as gratitude, forgiveness, and mindfulness. Delve into research findings that demonstrate how these practices can reduce stress, enhance emotional well-being, and promote overall mental health.

As you experience the concept of letting go as a process of surrendering control and releasing attachments to outcomes, fostering a sense of freedom and peace, you will learn practical techniques for practicing forgiveness, including self-forgiveness, and embracing a mindset of compassion toward oneself and others.

Experience the relationship between spirituality and inner peace, the importance of connecting with one's higher self, nature, or a divine source for guidance and solace. You will seek guidance by incorporating spiritual practices such as prayer, meditation, or rituals into daily life to deepen one's sense of inner harmony.

I have included a personal story that illustrates the transformative power of gratitude, forgiveness, and letting go in overcoming personal struggles and finding inner peace. This narrative can serve as an inspiring example of resilience and growth through spiritual practices.

Imagine Lillian, who faced deep personal struggles, including betrayal and loss. Through her spiritual practice, she embarked on a journey of resilience and growth, transforming her life in profound ways.

Power of Gratitude

Lillian began each day with a gratitude journal, focusing on blessings amidst challenges. By expressing gratitude for even small moments of beauty and kindness, she shifted her perspective and found solace during turmoil.

Forgiveness

Holding onto anger and resentment was weighing Lillian down, hindering her spiritual and emotional growth. Through deep introspection and meditation, she found the strength to forgive those who had hurt her, freeing herself from the burden of bitterness.

Letting Go

Lillian realized that holding onto the past was blocking her path to inner peace and growth. By practicing acceptance and letting go of what she couldn't change, she released the grip of painful memories and embraced the present moment with clarity and purpose.

Overcoming Personal Struggles

With newfound gratitude, forgiveness, and the ability to let go, Lillian faced her personal struggles with resilience and grace. She tackled each challenge head-on, drawing strength from her spiritual practices and unwavering belief in her ability to overcome adversity.

Finding Inner Peace

Through her journey of gratitude, forgiveness, and letting go, Lillian discovered a profound sense of inner peace. She radiated a newfound calm and serenity, embracing life with a renewed spirit of resilience, compassion, and joy.

Lillian is my mother's inspiring example that illustrates the transformative power of gratitude, forgiveness, and letting go in overcoming personal struggles and finding inner peace through spiritual practice. By cultivating these powerful qualities, she not only navigated through hardship but also emerged stronger, wiser, and more at peace with herself and the world around her. She would always say, "I won't complain."

Cultivating Your Inner Garden

In this chapter, we bring together the key teachings and practices from our journey of exploring *Gardening Your Mind with Spiritual Tools*. We reflect on the transformative power of self-awareness, intention-setting, nurturing growth, and harvesting inner peace by fostering personal well-being and spiritual growth.

By summarizing the core concepts of tending to our inner garden with mindfulness, intention, self-care, and gratitude, we emphasize the importance of cultivating a daily practice of self-reflection, compassion, and connection with the divine or higher self. We highlight how integrating these spiritual tools into our lives can lead to profound shifts in perception, behavior, and overall fulfillment.

I encourage readers to embark on their unique journey of self-discovery and inner cultivation, reminding them that the path to spiritual growth is a continuous process of learning, evolving, and embracing the present moment with an open heart and mind. By taking inspired action and embodying the practices shared in this book, readers can cultivate a life filled with purpose, joy, and inner peace.

GATEWAY TO CONNECTING TO A HIGHER CONSCIOUSNESS

Hopes of My Future Heaven Is Creating My Present Hades

Is the way I'm living bringing me some joy? Am I content with my present condition, or am I angry that God isn't giving me the things I desire on demand to be happy?

From a spiritual perspective, imagination can be seen as a gateway to connecting to a higher realm of consciousness, exploring deeper meanings, and envisioning spiritual growth and transformation. It can aid in visualizing intentions, manifestations, and spiritual goals. However, it is important to discern between imaginative visions and genuine spiritual experiences to avoid misconceptions or delusions. Cultivating a balanced approach that integrates imagination with mindfulness and spiritual practices can enhance your spiritual journey and inner growth.

What is required to feel good about the self is not the same from person to person. What you require for self-esteem is not necessarily what another person requires. It is important to discover what makes you feel worthy, confident, and happy about who you are.

Self-respect at the highest levels comes from honoring your soul. This means speaking and acting from a level of integrity and honesty that reflects your higher self. It means standing by what you believe in—you don't, however, have to convince others to believe in it—and acting in a way that reflects your values. Many of you criticize others for not living up to a value system you consider right, but on closer examination, you may not be living up to it yourself. You have seen the person who is always telling everyone how they should act, but he himself does anything he pleases (Roman, Living with Joy 1986).

Imagination can be a powerful tool for problem-solving and innovative thinking. It allows us to explore innovative ideas, envision possibilities, and think outside the box. In terms of personal development, it can foster empathy, understanding, and emotional intelligence. However, it is essential to balance imagination with critical thinking to ensure that our ideas are practical and realistic. Striking this balance can help harness the benefits of imagination while avoiding potential pitfalls.

When it comes to the pros of imagination, it can enhance creativity, problem-solving skills, and innovation. It also plays a crucial role in learning and personal development. However, on the flip side, excessive imagination without a grounding can lead to a disconnection from the present moment and potential difficulties in practical decision-making.

UNCERTAINTY: EVERY STORM IS NOT IN THE FORECAST

In the metaphorical garden of our minds, storms represent the unexpected challenges and difficulties that arise in life. Just as a gardener cannot predict every storm that might affect their garden, we too must accept that not all of life's challenges can be anticipated.

Unpredictable Weather Patterns

Despite our best efforts, weather forecasts are not always accurate. Similarly, life's events are not always foreseeable. We may face sudden storms of adversity, whether in the form of emotional upheaval, spiritual crises, or unexpected life events.

Acceptance and Preparedness

While we cannot control the timing or occurrence of these storms, we can cultivate a mindset of acceptance and readiness. By aligning ourselves with spiritual tools, such as mindfulness, resilience, and faith, we build an inner shelter that helps us withstand these unforeseen challenges.

Mindfulness helps me stay present and calm, even in the face of unexpected turmoil. Regular mindfulness practices, such as meditation, prepare us to navigate life's surprises with composure. Resilience allows us to bounce back from adversity. Like a well-tended plant that recovers from a storm, a resilient mindset helps us to regrow and flourish after setbacks. Having trust in the divine or a higher purpose can provide solace and perspective during challenging times. Faith acts as an anchor, grounding us when everything else feels chaotic.

Nurturing Your Inner Garden

Just as gardeners must adapt to changing weather conditions, we must be adaptable and resourceful in managing life's unpredictability. By nurturing our inner garden with spiritual tools, we cultivate inner strength and flexibility, enabling us to thrive even when the forecast is uncertain.

Practical Strategies

- Regular self-care: Routine practices that nurture your body, mind, and spirit ensure you're better prepared for life's unexpected challenges.
- Community support: Engaging with a supportive community provides additional resources and emotional support during times of crises.
- Continuous learning: Keep learning and implementing new spiritual tools and techniques to enhance your resilience and adaptability.

Conclusion

Every storm is not in the forecast, but by embracing this uncertainty with grace and preparedness, we cultivate a garden of the mind that is vibrant, resilient, and filled with the strength of spiritual healing. By accepting that not all challenges can be predicted, we open ourselves to growth and transformation, nurturing a garden that flourishes despite the unexpected.

SEED OF INSPIRATION

When I need a mental uplift, I plant a seed of inspiration from one of my favorite passages that for almost twenty-five years has been consistently misattributed to Nelson Mandela.

Marianne Williamson, author, self-help guru, and spiritual advisor to Oprah Winfrey, wrote one of her most famous pieces of rhetoric, a passage from her best-selling 1992 self-help book, *A Return to Love,* which often isn't attributed to her.

> Our deepest fear is not that we are inadequate, our deepest fear is that we are powerful beyond measure.
>
> It is our light, not our darkness, that most frightens us.
>
> You're playing small does not serve the world.
>
> There is nothing enlightened about shrinking
>
> so that other people won't feel insecure around you.

I can only refer to the quote because I tried getting copyright permission, but no one answered my text, email, physical letter, or calls. It is a stirring, inspirational passage tailor-made to remind people to be their best selves.

I spent most of my life being the victim of my own thoughts, my own emotions, and my own behaviors. I was consistently picking untrustworthy people to trust and unavailable people to love. I could not trust my own emotions because I was incapable of being honest with myself emotionally, which made me incapable of truly being honest on any level.

I had to become willing, open, and honest enough to start becoming conscious of the dysfunctional attitudes, the dysfunctional perspectives. I had to become willing to learn discernment in order to make choices about the changes I needed to make in my perspectives, especially my perspective on my own emotional process.

Once I started to feel the feelings, to do the grief work, I could begin to trust myself to be discerning about which of my emotions were telling me the truth. Only then was I able to substantially change my relationship with my God, myself, and life.

I learned that I was able to feel and release feelings without having them destroy me. I learned I could change my mental attitudes; I could change the way I think so my mind was no longer my worst enemy. I learned that by owning and honoring my feelings and their emotional wounds, I was able to take power away from those wounds by releasing the stored energy so I had choices over how I would respond instead of blindly reacting.

STOPPING THE WAR WITHIN

Don't Let Your Garden Become a Battlefield

When approaching a problem with a spiritually grounded mindset, consider the following steps:

1. Centering yourself: Take a moment to center yourself through meditation, prayer, or deep breathing. This can help you quiet your mind and connect with your inner wisdom.
2. Seeking clarity: Reflect on the problem at hand and try to gain a deeper understanding of its root causes and potential solutions. Journaling or discussing the problem with a trusted friend or mentor can help bring clarity.
3. Setting intentions: Set clear intentions for how you want to approach the problem and the outcome you wish to achieve. Let your spiritual beliefs guide you in setting positive and empowering intentions.
4. Practicing mindfulness: Stay present and mindful as you work toward solving the problem. Pay attention to your thoughts, emotions, and actions, and ensure they align with your spiritual values.
5. Seeking guidance: Draw inspiration and guidance from spiritual teachings, scriptures, or practices that resonate with you. They can offer insights and perspectives that may help you see the problem in a new light.

6. Taking inspired action: Trust your intuition and take action from a place of alignment with your spiritual beliefs. Listen to your inner guidance and take steps that feel right for you.
7. Embracing growth: View the problem as an opportunity for growth and learning. Trust that challenges are often opportunities in disguise, helping you evolve and deepen your spiritual practice.

By integrating these steps into your problem-solving process, you can create solutions that not only address the external issue but also nourish your spiritual well-being. Remember to be patient and compassionate with yourself throughout this journey.

Resolving Problems Beyond Their Origin

In the realm of personal growth and spiritual evolution, there exists a profound concept that some problems cannot be solved within the same frame of mind in which they were created. This notion calls upon individuals to transcend their current ways of thinking, feeling, and being to find true resolution and transformation. Here are examples that highlight the intricacies and challenges of solving problems from a higher perspective.

Example 1: Breaking Patterns of Self-Sabotage (Thought Patterns)

In this scenario, my current frame of mind, where I repeatedly find myself stuck in cycles of self-sabotage, unable to break free from destructive habits and in self-doubt and limiting beliefs, is the very breeding ground for my problems. To truly overcome this pattern, I had to elevate my consciousness, cultivate self-awareness, and embrace self-love and acceptance. By shifting to a mindset of empowerment and growth, I step out of the cycle of self-sabotage and create a new, more fulfilling reality. *Remember to be patient with yourself.*

Example 2: Healing Interpersonal Conflicts

Consider a situation where deep-seated conflicts and misunderstandings strain a relationship between two individuals. The discord and resentment that have accumulated over time cannot be resolved through the same communication patterns and perspectives that initially created them. Both parties must transcend their egos, practice empathy and active listening, and approach the conflict with a willingness to understand and forgive. By rising above their entrenched positions and opening their hearts to compassion and compromise, they can mend the broken bonds and forge a path toward reconciliation.

Example 3: Overcoming Existential Dilemmas

Delve into the existential realm, where individuals grapple with profound questions of purpose, meaning, and existence. When faced with existential crises that shake the very foundation of their being, attempting to find answers within the confines of their current worldview may prove futile. To navigate these turbulent waters, they must embark on a journey of self-discovery, introspection, and spiritual inquiry. By expanding their consciousness, embracing uncertainty, and seeking wisdom from various sources, they can transcend the limitations of their existing beliefs and find newfound clarity and peace.

Conclusion: The Path to Transcendence

In conclusion, the examples presented in this book underscore the transformative power of transcending the frames of mind in which problems are born. By daring to venture beyond familiar territory, embracing growth and self-discovery, and aligning with higher principles and truths, individuals can unravel the knots of unsolvable problems and emerge stronger, wiser, and more attuned to the infinite possibilities that await them. May this book inspire you to embark on your own journey of transcendence and unlock the boundless potential that lies within you.

As we conclude this journey together, I would like to express my gratitude for the opportunity to explore the depths of our inner landscapes and plant seeds of intention for a brighter, more aligned, and balanced future. May each reader find consolation in their participation to see identification, to embrace the education and enjoy the inspiration, to have the motivation to allow the transformation to start the celebration in living with joy that these teachings and practices presented, and may they continue to nurture their inner garden with love, compassion, and spiritual wisdom.

Remember, there's nothing going to happen today that you and God can't handle. God can't be the problem and the answer! So have a great day!

REFERENCES

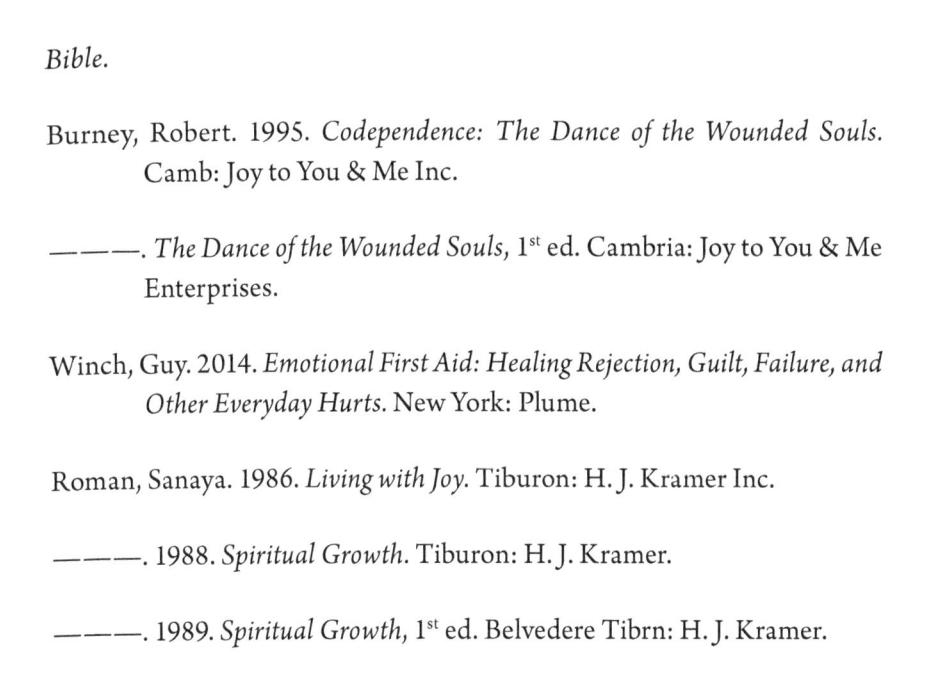

Bible.

Burney, Robert. 1995. *Codependence: The Dance of the Wounded Souls.* Camb: Joy to You & Me Inc.

———. *The Dance of the Wounded Souls*, 1st ed. Cambria: Joy to You & Me Enterprises.

Winch, Guy. 2014. *Emotional First Aid: Healing Rejection, Guilt, Failure, and Other Everyday Hurts.* New York: Plume.

Roman, Sanaya. 1986. *Living with Joy.* Tiburon: H. J. Kramer Inc.

———. 1988. *Spiritual Growth.* Tiburon: H. J. Kramer.

———. 1989. *Spiritual Growth*, 1st ed. Belvedere Tibrn: H. J. Kramer.